vegie food
low-fat & delicious

THE AUSTRALIAN
Women's Weekly

CONTENTS

Creating recipes that are both low in fat and have no meat, fowl or seafood content – but are still DELICIOUS – may sound a difficult brief, but we found ourselves pleasantly surprised at just how easy it was to develop this cookbook. Teaming the right vegetables with a carb or two and a complementary sauce or dressing proved to be a joy rather than a task, and the results are so yummy we think you'll love this book as much as we do.

Pamela Clark
Food Director

vegetables

are versatile, adaptable, full of nutrients and fibre, but low in fat and kilojoules, generally inexpensive, quick and easy to cook. And did we mention delicious? Whether because of a healthy lifestyle or ethical choice, more and more people have taken to eating a low-in-fat vegetarian diet: with the plethora of fresh vegies available, it's simple to cook tasty, nutritious meals and have a diet that's full of variety at the same time. A well-balanced vegetarian diet not only provides all the vitamins and minerals necessary for wellbeing, but it also lays the foundations for a long and healthy life-plan that contains no provision for obesity, coronary disease, high blood pressure, diabetes and even, possibly, some types of cancer. This book includes recipes that contain dairy products and eggs, as well as small, but healthy, amounts of oil – it's low-fat, remember, not no-fat, so nuts, seeds and avocados are definitely on the okay list. In fact, the more variety on the menu, the easier it is to fulfil the right dietary requirements, especially for protein. Since most plant foods (with the possible exception of soy and soy products such as tofu) only contain a few of the various elements that make up complete protein, it is vital that many different types of these, from legumes, pulses, whole grains, nuts and seeds, be consumed daily to reach the recommended daily nutritional intake.

Green (unripe) papayas are readily available in various sizes at many Asian food shops and markets. Select one that is very hard and slightly shiny, which indicates it's fresh but not too unripe to grate or chop.

pickled green papaya salad

preparation time 20 minutes (plus standing time) **cooking time** 5 minutes **serves 4**

1 cup (250ml) water

½ cup (125ml) rice vinegar

½ cup (110g) white sugar

1 teaspoon salt

1 fresh long red chilli, halved lengthways

1 small green papaya (650g)

150g sugar snap peas

100g bean thread noodles

½ small pineapple (450g), quartered, sliced thinly

1 small red onion (100g), sliced thinly

1 cup firmly packed fresh mint leaves

1 fresh long red chilli, sliced thinly

PALM SUGAR DRESSING

¼ cup (60ml) lime juice

2 tablespoons grated palm sugar

1 Combine the water, vinegar, sugar, salt and halved chilli in small saucepan; bring to a boil. Reduce heat; simmer, uncovered, 5 minutes. Strain into small jug; discard solids. Cool 10 minutes.

2 Meanwhile, peel papaya. Quarter lengthways, discard seeds. Grate papaya coarsely.

3 Place papaya in medium bowl with vinegar mixture, cover; stand 1 hour.

4 Meanwhile, boil, steam or microwave peas until just tender; drain. Place noodles in medium heatproof bowl, cover with boiling water; stand until just tender, drain. Rinse under cold water; drain. Using kitchen scissors, cut noodles into random lengths.

5 Place ingredients for palm sugar dressing in screw-top jar; shake well.

6 Place drained papaya, peas and noodles in medium bowl with pineapple, onion, mint and dressing; toss gently.

7 Divide salad between serving bowls; top with sliced chilli.
per serving 0.4g total fat (0.0g saturated fat); 577kJ (138 cal); 29g carbohydrate; 3.1g protein; 6.4g fibre

SALADS
FRESH, CLEAN-TASTING AND CRISP SALADS MAKE AN OUTSTANDING MAIN MEAL

BLACK-EYED BEAN SALAD

Cook two or three times the amount of beans called for in our recipe at right then, when cool, freeze what you don't use in one-cup portions. To make a quick salad, bring one portion of the frozen beans to room temperature. Toss them in a bowl with a quarter cup each of finely chopped red capsicum, celery and white onion. Sprinkle the mixture with a little bottled Italian dressing and serve in crisped iceberg lettuce-leaf cups. Also called black-eyed peas or cow peas, black-eyed beans can also be purchased canned and ready to use; these can be substituted for the dried variety called for in most recipes.

QUICK COLD SOBA

Cool the soba as described at right then chill in the refrigerator. Make a dressing with two tablespoons each of fresh lime juice and japanese soy sauce, a teaspoon each of grated fresh ginger and brown sugar, and two teaspoons of vegetable oil whisked together in a large bowl. Add two small carrots and two trimmed celery stalks, both cut into fine matchsticks, and the soba to bowl; toss to combine. Serve sprinkled with a finely shredded sheet of toasted nori.

black-eyed beans, tomato and rocket salad

preparation time 20 minutes cooking time 30 minutes serves 4

1 cup (200g) dried black-eyed beans

175g baby green beans, trimmed, chopped coarsely

1 medium red onion (170g), sliced thinly

250g cherry tomatoes, halved

250g yellow teardrop tomatoes, halved

100g baby rocket leaves

LEMON AND BASIL DRESSING

¼ cup (60ml) lemon juice

1 tablespoon olive oil

1 tablespoon dijon mustard

1 clove garlic, crushed

1 tablespoon finely chopped fresh basil

1 Cook black-eyed beans in medium saucepan of boiling water, uncovered, about 30 minutes or until just tender; drain. Rinse under cold water; drain.

2 Meanwhile, boil, steam or microwave green beans until just tender; drain. Rinse under cold water; drain.

3 Place ingredients for lemon and basil dressing in screw-top jar; shake well.

4 Place black-eyed beans and green beans in large bowl with remaining ingredients and dressing; toss gently.
per serving 6.1g total fat (0.8g saturated fat); 915kJ (219 cal); 26.3g carbohydrate; 15.3g protein; 11.2g fibre

soba and daikon salad

preparation time 20 minutes cooking time 15 minutes serves 4

300g dried soba noodles

1 small daikon (400g), cut into matchsticks

4 green onions, sliced thinly

1 teaspoon sesame oil

100g enoki mushrooms

2 tablespoons thinly sliced pickled ginger

1 toasted seaweed sheet (yaki-nori), sliced thinly

MIRIN DRESSING

¼ cup (60ml) mirin

2 tablespoons kecap manis

1 tablespoon sake

1 clove garlic, crushed

1cm piece fresh ginger (5g), grated

1 teaspoon white sugar

1 Cook soba in large saucepan of boiling water, uncovered, until just tender; drain. Rinse under cold water; drain.

2 Place ingredients for mirin dressing in screw-top jar; shake well.

3 Place soba in large bowl with daikon, onion and half of the dressing; toss gently.

4 Heat oil in small frying pan; cook mushrooms, stirring, 2 minutes.

5 Divide soba salad among serving plates; top with combined mushrooms, ginger and seaweed. Drizzle with remaining dressing.
per serving 2.4g total fat (0.3g saturated fat); 1292kJ (309 cal); 56.6g carbohydrate; 10.9g protein; 5.3g fibre

We used the sun-dried tomatoes
that have not been preserved in
oil, which are generally sold in
plastic bags or loose by weight.

italian brown rice salad

preparation time 15 minutes cooking time 1 hour serves 4

3 cups (750ml) vegetable stock

2 teaspoons olive oil

1 small brown onion (80g), chopped finely

1½ cups (300g) brown medium-grain rice

1 teaspoon finely grated lime rind

1 clove garlic, crushed

⅓ cup (45g) toasted slivered almonds

⅔ cup (100g) sun-dried tomatoes, chopped coarsely

½ cup (60g) seeded black olives, chopped coarsely

½ cup coarsely chopped fresh basil

¼ cup coarsely chopped fresh flat-leaf parsley

LIME AND MUSTARD DRESSING

2 tablespoons lime juice

2 tablespoons white wine vinegar

2 cloves garlic, crushed

2 teaspoons dijon mustard

1   Place stock in medium saucepan; bring to a boil. Reduce heat;
    simmer, covered.

2   Meanwhile, heat oil in large saucepan; cook onion, stirring, until
    soft. Add rice, rind and garlic; stir to coat rice in onion mixture.

3   Add stock; bring to a boil. Reduce heat; simmer, covered, about
    50 minutes or until rice is tender and liquid is absorbed.

4   Place ingredients for lime and mustard dressing in screw-top jar;
    shake well.

5   Add remaining ingredients and dressing to rice mixture in pan;
    toss gently to combine.

6   Serve salad warm; top with fresh flat-leaf parsley, if desired.
    per serving 13.3 g total fat (1.8g saturated fat); 1923kJ (460 cal);
    76.3g carbohydrate; 14.7g protein; 9.4g fibre

CRISP FRIED NOODLES

Sold in cellophane bags or cans ready
to use, deep-fried wheat-flour noodles
can be eaten straight from the pack as
a snack, used as the base for chocolate
peanut spiders or served instead of rice
with stir-fries. You can make your own
by deep-frying bean thread, dried wheat
or even fresh thin rice noodles, in small
batches, and using them as a bed for a
vegetarian larb (salad) or tofu sang choy
bow (a spicy minced mixture wrapped
and served in a lettuce leaf).

BROAD BEANS

Fresh broad beans, also known as fava
beans, are flat, slightly-kidney-shaped
legumes encased in hard shells growing
inside fuzzy long green pods. The pods
are discarded before cooking, but the
shells after, to help retain the inner bean's
nutrients, sweet flavour and tender texture.
Frozen broad beans can be substituted
when fresh are out of season; they can be
used as they are, but are much sweeter if
the outer shell is removed. Delicious on
their own, broad beans are good pureed
into dips or pestos, and go well with
pistachios, mint, lemon and parmesan.

asian crispy noodle salad

preparation time 15 minutes serves 4

½ medium chinese cabbage (500g), shredded finely

227g can water chestnuts, drained, sliced thinly

150g snow peas, trimmed, sliced thinly

1 large red capsicum (350g), sliced thinly

100g packet fried noodles

⅓ cup (50g) toasted unsalted cashews, chopped coarsely

1 cup loosely packed fresh coriander leaves

SESAME SOY DRESSING

1 teaspoon sesame oil

¼ cup (60ml) soy sauce

1 tablespoon sweet chilli sauce

2 tablespoons lime juice

1 Place ingredients for sesame soy dressing in screw-top jar; shake well.

2 Combine cabbage, water chestnuts, snow peas, capsicum and fried noodles in medium bowl.

3 Divide salad among serving bowls; sprinkle with nuts and coriander, drizzle with dressing.
per serving 10.8g fat (2.2g saturated fat); 869kJ (208 cal); 19.1g carbohydrate; 8.3g protein; 6.4g fibre

broad bean and risoni salad with cherry tomatoes

preparation time 45 minutes cooking time 30 minutes serves 4

If you cannot buy fresh, use 500g frozen broad beans.

1kg fresh broad beans, shelled

250g risoni

1 tablespoon olive oil

3 green onions, sliced thinly

2 cloves garlic, sliced thinly

1 cup coarsely chopped fresh mint

¼ cup (60ml) lemon juice

500g cherry tomatoes, halved

1 tablespoon brown sugar

1 cup (80g) shaved parmesan

1 Boil, steam or microwave beans until just tender; drain. Rinse under cold water; drain. Peel away grey-coloured outer shells.

2 Cook risoni in medium saucepan of boiling water, uncovered, until just tender; drain.

3 Meanwhile, heat oil in large frying pan; cook onion and garlic, stirring, until onion softens. Add risoni, beans, mint and juice; stir until combined. Transfer to large serving platter.

4 Cook tomato and sugar in same frying pan, stirring occasionally, about 5 minutes or until tomato just softens.

5 Top risoni salad with tomato; sprinkle with cheese.
per serving 12.9g total fat (5.1g saturated fat); 1864kJ (446 cal); 53.3g carbohydrate; 27.5g protein; 15.8g fibre

burghul salad with chickpeas

preparation time 20 minutes cooking time 10 minutes serves 4

1 large red capsicum (350g)

1 cup (160g) burghul

1 cup (250ml) boiling water

420g can chickpeas, rinsed, drained

1 trimmed celery stalk (100g), chopped finely

50g baby spinach leaves

SUMAC AND HERB DRESSING

1 tablespoon sesame seeds

2 tablespoons sumac

1 tablespoon fresh thyme leaves

1 tablespoon coarsely chopped fresh oregano

½ cup (125ml) lime juice

1 tablespoon olive oil

1 clove garlic, crushed

1 Quarter capsicum; discard seeds and membranes. Roast under grill or in very hot oven, skin-side up, until skin blisters and blackens. Cover capsicum pieces with plastic or paper for 5 minutes; peel away skin, then slice capsicum thinly.

2 Meanwhile, place burghul in medium bowl, cover with the boiling water; stand about 10 minutes or until burghul softens and water is absorbed.

3 Combine ingredients for sumac and herb dressing in small bowl.

4 Place burghul and capsicum in large bowl with chickpeas, celery, spinach and dressing; toss gently.
   per serving 8.6g total fat (1.2g saturated fat); 1150kJ (275 cal); 37.3g carbohydrate; 11.2g protein; 11.8g fibre

SAUCE OF THE NEW SEASON

The word "primavera" means spring
in Italian, and it's traditional in Italy for
cooks to use the youngest and best of
the new season's produce in this pasta
sauce. Other than that, there are no
fixed ideas on what it can or cannot
contain. You'll find that no two recipes
are alike, except for the fact that they
smack of the freshness of spring. Some
may also contain toasted pine nuts, still
others lashings of cream, but they're
all usually served over a long pasta like
spaghetti, fettuccine or linguine.

SALSA, GUACAMOLE & CHIPS

Here's a simple but tasty suggestion
for nibblies with drinks: make the
fresh tomato salsa by following the
instructions in step 2 at right (but
omitting the beans); divide salsa
between two small serving bowls. Use
the back of a fork to roughly mash a
small, ripe, coarsely chopped avocado
into one bowl of the salsa. Serve the
bowls of salsa and guacamole with corn
tortilla chips... and margaritas, of course!

pasta primavera

preparation time 15 minutes cooking time 20 minutes serves 4

375g penne

200g baby carrots, quartered lengthways

350g asparagus, trimmed, cut into 4cm lengths

150g snow peas, trimmed, halved

1 cup (120g) frozen peas

4 green onions, sliced thinly

2 medium egg tomatoes (150g), seeded, chopped finely

LEMON THYME AND MUSTARD DRESSING

1 tablespoon dijon mustard

1 tablespoon white wine vinegar

1 tablespoon lemon juice

2 tablespoons water

2 tablespoons coarsely chopped fresh lemon thyme

1 tablespoon olive oil

1   Cook pasta in large saucepan of boiling water, uncovered, until just tender; drain. Rinse under cold water; drain.

2   Meanwhile, boil, steam or microwave carrot, asparagus and peas, separately, until tender; drain. Rinse under cold water; drain.

3   Place ingredients for lemon thyme and mustard dressing in screw-top jar; shake well.

4   Place pasta and vegetables in large bowl with onion, tomato and dressing; toss gently.

per serving 6.1g total fat (0.8g saturated fat); 1747kJ (418 cal); 73.1g carbohydrate; 16.5g protein; 9g fibre

mexican bean salad with tortilla chips

preparation time 20 minutes cooking time 5 minutes serves 4

4 medium tomatoes (600g), seeded, chopped coarsely

420g can four-bean mix, rinsed, drained

300g can kidney beans, rinsed, drained

½ cup coarsely chopped fresh coriander

¼ cup (60ml) lime juice

1 small red onion (100g), chopped finely

2 fresh long red chillies, chopped finely

4 small flour tortillas, cut into wedges

1 small avocado (200g)

2 tablespoons light sour cream

1   Preheat oven to moderately hot (200°C/180°C fan-forced).

2   Combine tomato, beans, ⅓ cup of the coriander, 1 tablespoon of the juice, half of the onion and half of the chilli in medium bowl.

3   Place tortilla wedges, in single layer, on oven tray; toast about 5 minutes or until crisp.

4   Meanwhile, to make guacamole, mash avocado in small bowl; stir in remaining coriander, juice, onion and chilli.

5   Divide tortilla chips among plates; top with bean mixture, guacamole and sour cream.

per serving 14g total fat (3.7g saturated fat); 1522kJ (364 cal); 44.9g carbohydrate; 14.1g protein; 10.9g fibre

Wonton wrappers can be found in the refrigerated sections of most supermarkets or Asian grocery stores.

kumara and romano ravioli with tomato and basil sauce

preparation time 20 minutes **cooking time** 25 minutes **serves** 4

1 large kumara (500g), chopped coarsely

2 tablespoons finely grated romano cheese

1 tablespoon dried currants

40 wonton wrappers

1 egg white, beaten lightly

TOMATO AND BASIL SAUCE

2 teaspoons olive oil

1 medium brown onion (150g), sliced thinly

½ cup (125ml) dry white wine

3 large egg tomatoes (270g), seeded, chopped finely

¼ cup (60ml) vegetable stock

1 tablespoon finely chopped fresh basil

1   Boil, steam or microwave kumara until tender; drain. Mash in medium bowl until smooth. Stir in cheese and currants.

2   Meanwhile, make tomato and basil sauce.

3   Place 1 tablespoon of the kumara mixture in centre of each of 20 wonton wrappers; brush around edge with egg white. Top each with a remaining wrapper, press around edges firmly to seal.

4   Cook ravioli, in batches, in large saucepan of boiling water, uncovered, about 4 minutes or until ravioli float to the surface.

5   Serve ravioli topped with tomato and basil sauce, sprinkled with fresh basil leaves and served with a baby rocket and parmesan salad, if desired.

TOMATO AND BASIL SAUCE Heat oil in medium frying pan; cook onion, stirring, until onion softens. Add wine; bring to a boil. Reduce heat; simmer, uncovered, until wine has almost evaporated. Add tomato and stock; stir until heated through. Stir in basil.

per serving 4.5g total fat (1.2g saturated fat); 1580kJ (374 cal); 64.6g carbohydrate; 14g protein; 3.1g fibre

STIR-FRIES & PAN-FRIES
A WELL-SEASONED WOK OR FRYING PAN TAKES THE FEAR OUT OF FRYING

asparagus, mushroom and lemon pilaf

preparation time 15 minutes cooking time 45 minutes serves 4

20g butter

1 tablespoon vegetable oil

1 large red onion (300g), chopped finely

3 cloves garlic, crushed

200g swiss brown mushrooms, quartered

1½ cups (300g) basmati rice

½ cup (100g) red lentils

¾ cup (180ml) dry white wine

1½ cups (375ml) vegetable stock

2 teaspoons finely grated lemon rind

2 tablespoons lemon juice

2¼ cups (560ml) water

300g asparagus, trimmed

¼ cup loosely packed fresh lemon thyme leaves

1 tablespoon toasted flaked almonds

1 Heat butter and oil in large saucepan; cook onion and garlic, stirring, until onion softens. Add mushrooms; cook, stirring, until just tender. Stir in rice and lentils; cook, stirring, 1 minute. Add wine; cook, stirring, until liquid is absorbed.

2 Add stock, rind, juice and 2 cups of the water; bring to a boil. Reduce heat; simmer, uncovered, stirring occasionally, about 20 minutes or until liquid is absorbed and rice is just tender.

3 Meanwhile, cut asparagus in half lengthways, then in half crossways.

4 Stir asparagus, half of the thyme and remaining water into pilaf; cook, covered, over low heat, about 5 minutes or until asparagus is tender.

5 Divide pilaf among serving plates; sprinkle with nuts and remaining thyme.
per serving 11.3g total fat (3.4g saturated fat); 2082kJ (498 cal); 74.1g carbohydrate; 16.6g protein; 9g fibre

GAI LARN, YUM CHA STYLE

One of the most popular chinese vegetables, gai larn or chinese kale, is distinguished by its dark green leaves, sturdy edible stems and small flowers. Recreate the way it's served at Sunday yum cha: discard any dry outer leaves then chop a bunch of gai larn in half crossways; par-boil only long enough to slightly soften the stems. Drain, and splash with a little sesame oil and oyster sauce to serve (note that there is a "vegetarian" oyster sauce available made from blended mushrooms and soy).

MINI MEZZE IN A MINUTE

Friends coming by and you're just leaving work? Stop at a good deli and pick up some marinated fetta, two different kinds of olives and a package of grissini. Once home, make a beetroot dip by draining a small can of whole baby beetroot and processing it with a tablespoon or so from a 500g tub of greek-style yogurt, a similar amount of tahini, the juice of a lemon and one crushed garlic clove. To make tzatziki, peel and seed then finely chop two small cucumbers; stir it into remaining tub of yogurt with crushed garlic, and salt and pepper to taste. Place the beetroot dip, tzatziki, fetta and olives in separate bowls, stand the grissini upright in a tall container, open the wine... and relax.

26

stir-fried asian greens in black bean sauce

preparation time 10 minutes cooking time 15 minutes serves 4

2 cups (400g) jasmine rice

1 tablespoon peanut oil

150g sugar snap peas, trimmed

400g gai larn, chopped coarsely

200g snake beans, trimmed, cut into 5cm lengths

2 cloves garlic, sliced thinly

1 fresh small red thai chilli, chopped finely

2 medium zucchini (240g), sliced thickly

2 tablespoons black bean sauce

1 tablespoon kecap manis

1 teaspoon sesame oil

⅓ cup (50g) toasted unsalted cashews, chopped coarsely

1 Cook rice in large saucepan of boiling water, uncovered, until just tender; drain.

2 Meanwhile, heat peanut oil in wok; stir-fry peas, gai larn stems, beans, garlic, chilli and zucchini until stems are just tender.

3 Add sauces, sesame oil, gai larn leaves and nuts; stir-fry until leaves are just wilted.

4 Serve stir-fry with rice.

per serving 13.3g total fat (2.6g saturated fat); 2274kJ (544 cal); 89.5g carbohydrate; 15.4g protein; 8.8g fibre

pan-fried tofu with beetroot hummus

preparation time 15 minutes cooking time 30 minutes serves 4

1 medium beetroot (175g)

4 small red onions (400g), quartered

420g can chickpeas, drained, rinsed

2 cloves garlic, quartered

¼ cup (60ml) lemon juice

3 teaspoons tahini

300g firm tofu, diced into 3cm pieces

2 tablespoons sumac

100g baby spinach leaves

100g rocket

1 Peel beetroot; cut into thin wedges.

2 Heat medium lightly oiled non-stick frying pan; cook onion, stirring occasionally, until just tender. Transfer to large bowl.

3 Cook beetroot in same pan, covered, about 15 minutes or until tender.

4 Meanwhile, cook chickpeas in small saucepan of boiling water, uncovered, about 10 minutes or until chickpeas are just tender; drain, reserving ¼ cup of the cooking liquid.

5 Blend or process beetroot, chickpeas, reserved cooking liquid, garlic, juice and tahini until smooth.

6 Combine tofu and sumac in medium bowl; cook tofu, in batches, in same cleaned lightly oiled frying pan until browned all over.

7 Add spinach and rocket to onion in large bowl; toss gently. Serve onion mixture topped with tofu and beetroot hummus.

per serving 9.6g total fat (1.3g saturated fat); 995kJ (238 cal); 20.4g carbohydrate; 17.7g protein; 9g fibre

lemon and dill risotto cakes

preparation time 20 minutes cooking time 1 hour (plus refrigeration time) serves 6

2 cups (500ml) vegetable stock

3 cups (750ml) water

1 tablespoon olive oil

1 medium brown onion (150g), chopped finely

2 cloves garlic, crushed

2 cups (400g) arborio rice

1 cup (250ml) dry white wine

1 tablespoon finely grated lemon rind

2 tablespoons finely chopped fresh dill

2 radicchio (400g), chopped coarsely

LEMON DILL DRESSING

1 tablespoon lemon juice

2 tablespoons finely chopped fresh dill

1 tablespoon olive oil

1 tablespoon cider vinegar

1 tablespoon dijon mustard

1 Place stock and the water in medium saucepan; bring to a boil. Reduce heat, simmer, covered.

2 Meanwhile, heat oil in large saucepan; cook onion and garlic, stirring, until soft. Add rice; stir to coat rice in onion mixture. Add wine; cook, stirring, until liquid is absorbed. Add ½ cup of the simmering stock; cook, stirring, over low heat until stock is absorbed. Continue adding stock, in ½-cup batches, stirring, until stock is absorbed after each addition. Total cooking time should be about 35 minutes or until rice is tender. Stir in rind and dill. Cool risotto 10 minutes. Cover; refrigerate 2 hours.

3 Combine ingredients for lemon dill dressing in small bowl.

4 Shape risotto into 18 risotto cakes. Heat large lightly oiled frying pan; cook cakes, in batches, until browned lightly both sides. Cover to keep warm.

5 Cook radicchio, stirring, in same pan until just wilted.

6 Serve risotto cakes with radicchio, drizzled with dressing.
per serving 7.2g total fat (1g saturated fat); 1421kJ (340 cal); 55.3g carbohydrate; 6.2g protein; 3.6g fibre

Chickpea flour is usually sold in Indian food shops by the name of besan.

A raita is any dip or accompaniment having yogurt as its main ingredient and any of a great number of different vegies, nuts, herbs or spices stirred in for flavour.

onion and spinach pakoras with cucumber raita

preparation time 20 minutes cooking time 30 minutes makes 16

2 cups (300g) chickpea flour

2 large uncooked potatoes (600g), grated coarsely

2 large brown onions (400g), sliced thinly

100g baby spinach leaves, chopped coarsely

4 cloves garlic, crushed

1 teaspoon chilli powder

½ teaspoon ground cumin

1 teaspoon salt

¼ teaspoon ground turmeric

1 teaspoon garam masala

¼ teaspoon baking powder

¼ cup coarsely chopped fresh mint

¼ cup (60ml) water

2 tablespoons olive oil

CUCUMBER RAITA

1 lebanese cucumber (130g), grated coarsely

200g low-fat yogurt

¼ cup (60ml) lemon juice

¼ cup coarsely chopped fresh mint

1   Using hand, combine all ingredients except the oil, in medium bowl.
2   Shape ¼ cups of the potato mixture into patties. Heat oil in large frying pan; cook pakoras, in batches, about 10 minutes or until browned lightly both sides.
3   Meanwhile, combine ingredients for cucumber raita in small bowl.
4   Serve pakoras with raita.
    per serving 2.8g total fat (0.4g saturated fat); 489kJ (117 cal); 17.9g carbohydrate; 4.4g protein; 3.4g fibre

You need to cook about 2 cups of jasmine rice the day before you want to make this – or any fried rice recipe. Spread the rice out in a thin layer on a tray, cover, and refrigerate overnight.

nasi goreng

preparation time 20 minutes cooking time 15 minutes serves 4

1 small brown onion (80g), chopped coarsely

2 cloves garlic, quartered

5cm piece fresh ginger (25g), chopped coarsely

2 fresh long red chillies, chopped coarsely

1 tablespoon peanut oil

4 eggs, beaten lightly

150g oyster mushrooms, chopped coarsely

1 medium green capsicum (200g), chopped coarsely

1 medium red capsicum (200g), chopped coarsely

200g fresh baby corn, chopped coarsely

4 cups cooked jasmine rice

1 cup (80g) bean sprouts

3 green onions, sliced thinly

2 tablespoons soy sauce

1 tablespoon kecap manis

1 Blend or process brown onion, garlic, ginger and chilli until almost smooth.
2 Heat 1 teaspoon of the oil in wok; add half of the egg, swirl wok to make thin omelette. Cook, uncovered, until egg is just set. Remove from wok; cut into thick strips. Repeat process with another 1 teaspoon of the oil and remaining egg.
3 Heat remaining oil in same wok; stir-fry onion mixture until fragrant. Add mushrooms, capsicums and corn; stir-fry until tender.
4 Add rice, sprouts, green onion and sauces; stir-fry until heated through.
5 Serve nasi goreng topped with omelette.
per serving 11.2g total fat (2.5g saturated fat); 1843kJ (441 cal); 66.8g carbohydrate; 17.6g protein; 7.2g fibre

THREE-PEA SALAD

Cook the same amounts of the three
peas shown at right and refresh
immediately under cold water. Drain,
then toss them in a bowl with the juice
of a lemon, a quarter of a cup each of
finely chopped fresh mint and chives.
Perfect with a simple cheese soufflé
and a baguette for a light lunch.

A LOOK AT PAELLA

While paella (pronounced pie-ay-ya) is
practically the national dish of Spain,
its origins are in that country's Islamic
past, when growing rice and cooking it
in a shallow open pan was introduced
by the Arabs of North Africa. It is
traditionally made with calasparra, a fine
short-grain rice grown in the central east
of Spain, near Valencia, the city most
identified with paella. Like arborio, this
rice doesn't have a tendency to clump
and is almost impossible to overcook.
After the type of rice and shape of the
pan, the other most important part of a
true paella is the inclusion of real saffron.

angel hair pasta with peas and ricotta

preparation time 15 minutes cooking time 15 minutes serves 4

375g angel hair pasta

150g sugar snap peas, trimmed

150g snow peas, trimmed

½ cup (60g) frozen peas

1 tablespoon olive oil

1 medium red onion (170g), sliced thinly

2 cloves garlic, crushed

2 tablespoons drained baby capers, rinsed

½ cup (125ml) lemon juice

½ cup coarsely chopped fresh mint

½ cup coarsely chopped fresh flat-leaf parsley

200g low-fat ricotta, crumbled

1 Cook pasta in large saucepan of boiling water, uncovered, until just tender; drain.

2 Meanwhile, boil, steam or microwave peas until just tender; drain. Rinse under cold water; drain.

3 Heat oil in large saucepan; cook onion, garlic and capers, stirring, 2 minutes. Add pasta; cook, stirring, 3 minutes. Place pasta mixture, peas, juice and herbs in large bowl; toss gently.

4 Serve pasta topped with cheese.

per serving 10.4g total fat (3.7g saturated fat); 1990kJ (476 cal); 73.9g carbohydrate; 20.1g protein; 7.5g fibre

vegetarian paella

preparation time 25 minutes cooking time 55 minutes serves 4

3 cups (750ml) vegetable stock

2 cups (500ml) water

pinch saffron threads

1 tablespoon olive oil

2 baby eggplants (120g), quartered

2 cloves garlic, crushed

1 medium red onion (170g), chopped finely

2 medium tomatoes (300g), seeded, chopped finely

1 medium red capsicum (200g), chopped finely

2 teaspoons smoked paprika

1¾ cups (350g) arborio rice

1 cup (120g) frozen peas

100g green beans, trimmed, chopped coarsely

½ cup (60g) seeded black olives

¼ cup finely chopped fresh flat-leaf parsley

1 Heat stock and the water in medium saucepan; bring to a boil. Remove from heat; stir in saffron.

2 Heat oil in large frying pan; cook eggplant, stirring occasionally, about 5 minutes or until browned. Remove from pan.

3 Cook garlic, onion, tomato, capsicum and paprika in same pan, stirring, until onion softens. Add rice; stir to coat in mixture. Stir in stock mixture; bring to a boil. Reduce heat; simmer, uncovered, about 20 minutes or until rice is almost tender.

4 Sprinkle peas, beans and eggplant evenly over surface of paella; simmer, covered, about 10 minutes or until beans and rice are tender. Sprinkle with olives and parsley; stand, covered, 5 minutes before serving.

per serving 6.4g total fat (1.2g saturated fat); 1839kJ (440 cal); 82.4g carbohydrate; 12.4g protein; 5.9g fibre

spanish omelette with tomato salsa

preparation time 20 minutes cooking time 55 minutes serves 6

2 large potatoes (600g), sliced thinly

2 medium brown onions (300g), sliced thinly

1 medium red capsicum (200g), chopped coarsely

150g green beans, trimmed, chopped coarsely

8 eggs

¼ cup (60ml) skim milk

⅓ cup coarsely chopped fresh flat-leaf parsley

TOMATO SALSA

1 large tomato (220g), seeded, chopped finely

2 lebanese cucumbers (260g), seeded, chopped finely

1 small red onion (100g), chopped finely

2 long green chillies, chopped finely

¼ cup (60ml) lemon juice

2 tablespoons finely chopped fresh coriander

1   Heat lightly oiled 26cm frying pan; cook potato and onion, stirring, 2 minutes. Reduce heat; cook, covered, stirring occasionally, 15 minutes. Add capsicum and beans; cook, covered, about 5 minutes or until potato is tender. Remove from heat.

2   Whisk eggs, milk and parsley in large jug. Pour over potato mixture; stir gently.

3   Return pan to low heat; cook, uncovered, 20 minutes. Cover; cook about 10 minutes or until omelette is cooked.

4   Meanwhile, combine ingredients for tomato salsa in small bowl.

5   Serve omelette topped with salsa.
    per serving 7.4g total fat (2.2g saturated fat); 1672kJ (200 cal); 18.7g carbohydrate; 14.1g protein; 4.5g fibre

five-spice tofu with egg noodles and lemon chilli sauce

preparation time 15 minutes cooking time 25 minutes serves 4

½ cup (125ml) sweet chilli sauce

2 teaspoons finely grated lemon rind

¼ cup (60ml) lemon juice

440g packet fresh egg noodles

⅓ cup (50g) plain flour

2 teaspoons five-spice powder

300g firm tofu, diced into 2cm pieces

1 tablespoon olive oil

1 large brown onion (200g), chopped coarsely

3 cloves garlic, sliced thinly

1 small yellow capsicum (150g), sliced thinly

300g sugar snap peas, trimmed

1 Combine sauce, rind and juice in small saucepan; bring to a boil. Remove from heat.

2 Place noodles in large heatproof bowl; cover with boiling water, separate with fork, drain.

3 Combine flour and five-spice in medium bowl, add tofu; toss to coat tofu in flour mixture.

4 Heat half of the oil in wok; cook tofu, in batches, until browned all over.

5 Heat remaining oil in wok; stir-fry onion, garlic and capsicum until onion softens. Add noodles, peas and half of the lemon chilli sauce; stir-fry until peas are just tender.

6 Serve noodles topped with tofu and drizzled with remaining lemon chilli sauce.

per serving 12.2g total fat (1.8g saturated fat); 2241kJ (536 cal); 80.3g carbohydrate; 24.6g protein; 8.5g fibre

Also known as dried wood ear, black fungus is popular in Asian cooking. Black on one side and pale grey on the other, this fungus has to be soaked before use. It swells to about five times the dried size when rehydrated. Any dried mushroom can be substituted for the black fungus called for here if necessary, but it's readily available from Asian food shops.

rice noodles with brussels sprouts

preparation time 20 minutes (plus standing time) cooking time 15 minutes serves 4

10g dried black fungus

8 dried shiitake mushrooms

450g fresh rice noodles

2 teaspoons peanut oil

1 clove garlic, crushed

5cm piece fresh ginger (25g), grated

1 large red capsicum (350g), sliced thinly

300g brussels sprouts, quartered

½ cup (125ml) water

2 tablespoons soy sauce

1 tablespoon kecap manis

½ cup (125ml) vegetable stock

½ cup loosely packed fresh mint leaves

1 Place fungus and mushrooms in medium heatproof bowl; cover with boiling water. Stand 20 minutes; drain. Discard mushroom stems; slice caps and fungus thickly.

2 Place noodles in large heatproof bowl; cover with boiling water, separate with fork, drain.

3 Heat oil in wok; stir-fry garlic and ginger until fragrant. Add capsicum, sprouts, fungus and mushrooms; stir-fry 2 minutes. Add the water; cook, covered, about 5 minutes or until vegetables are tender. Add noodles, sauces and stock; stir-fry until heated through. Stir in mint.
per serving 3.8g total fat (0.5g saturated fat); 1200kJ (287 cal); 52.4g carbohydrate; 9.9g protein; 5.5g fibre

THE FRIENDLY FRITTATA

Almost as perfect a package as the egg itself, a frittata can be eaten hot or cold, served as an elegant light meal or hand-held snack, cooked in the oven or on top the stove, and be individually tailored according to your taste buds' desire. The difference in an Italian frittata and a French omelette is more then just a matter of origin. A frittata has the filling content mixed in with the beaten eggs before cooking while an omelette is traditionally folded over the filling in the pan. Frittatas can be served at room temperature, making them perfect for picnics or lunch boxes, while an omelette is almost always eaten hot.

EASY ANTIPASTI

Scatter baby rocket leaves over the surface of a large serving platter then top with equal-sized amounts of semi-dried tomatoes, bocconcini, smoked mozzarella, marinated mushrooms, and char-grilled eggplant and capsicum pieces. Serve with lightly toasted sliced ciabatta before an Italian main course.

42

leek frittata with baby spinach salad

preparation time 15 minutes cooking time 25 minutes serves 4

You need a medium frying pan with a 19cm base for this recipe.

6 eggs

½ cup (125ml) light evaporated milk

20g butter

1 medium leek (350g), sliced thinly

⅔ cup (80g) frozen peas

2 medium tomatoes (300g), sliced thinly

2 tablespoons finely grated parmesan

80g baby spinach leaves

250g yellow grape tomatoes, halved

½ small red onion (50g), sliced thinly

2 teaspoons olive oil

1 teaspoon red wine vinegar

1 Preheat grill.
2 Combine eggs and milk in large jug.
3 Heat butter in medium frying pan; cook leek, stirring, until softened. Add peas, sliced tomato and egg mixture; cook, uncovered, over low heat until frittata is almost set. Remove from heat; sprinkle with cheese.
4 Place under grill until frittata sets and top is browned lightly. Stand frittata in pan 5 minutes before cutting into wedges.
5 Meanwhile, place remaining ingredients in medium bowl; toss gently.
6 Serve frittata with salad.
   per serving 15.9g total fat (6.2g saturated fat); 1078kJ (258 cal); 11.1g carbohydrate; 17.9g protein; 5.3g fibre

pan-fried haloumi with green salad

preparation time 15 minutes cooking time 5 minutes serves 4

Haloumi must be cooked just before serving or it becomes leathery and unpalatable.

150g curly endive

50g baby spinach leaves

½ cup loosely packed fresh flat-leaf parsley leaves

⅔ cup (125g) drained semi-dried tomatoes, chopped coarsely

250g haloumi cheese

LEMON DIJON DRESSING

¼ cup (60ml) lemon juice

1 clove garlic, crushed

1 tablespoon water

1 teaspoon white sugar

1 teaspoon dijon mustard

¼ teaspoon ground cumin

pinch cayenne pepper

1 Combine endive, spinach, parsley and tomato in medium bowl.
2 Cut cheese into eight slices.
3 Heat lightly oiled medium frying pan; cook cheese, in batches, until browned both sides.
4 Meanwhile, place ingredients for lemon dijon dressing in screw-top jar; shake well.
5 Add dressing to salad; toss gently. Serve salad topped with cheese.
   per serving 12g fat (7g saturated fat); 949kJ (227 cal); 11.8g carbohydrate; 17.3g protein; 5.4g fibre

The chilli tomato relish is best made a day or two ahead, to allow the flavours to marry. You can add a finely chopped fresh red thai chilli to the mixture if you want it hotter. Keep, covered, in the refrigerator.

lentil and bean burger with tomato chilli relish

preparation time 20 minutes   cooking time 25 minutes (plus refrigeration and cooling time)   serves 4

1 cup (200g) red lentils

420g can four-bean mix, rinsed, drained

1 egg

4 green onions, chopped coarsely

2 tablespoons coarsely chopped fresh coriander

4 hamburger buns

8 butter lettuce leaves

40g bean sprouts

40g snow pea sprouts, trimmed

1 lebanese cucumber (130g), sliced thinly

CHILLI TOMATO RELISH

2 medium tomatoes (300g), chopped coarsely

1 small brown onion (80g), chopped finely

1 clove garlic, crushed

⅓ cup (80ml) sweet chilli sauce

2 tablespoons malt vinegar

1   Make chilli tomato relish.

2   Meanwhile, cook lentils in medium saucepan of boiling water until tender; drain. Cool 10 minutes.

3   Blend or process lentils, beans and egg until mixture forms a smooth paste. Combine in medium bowl with onion and coriander; cover, refrigerate 1 hour.

4   Using floured hands, shape lentil mixture into four patties; cook patties in large heated lightly oiled non-stick frying pan until browned both sides and heated through. Remove from pan; cover to keep warm.

5   Split buns in half; toast cut-sides of buns. Spread buns with relish; sandwich lettuce, sprouts, cucumber, patties and remaining relish between buns.

CHILLI TOMATO RELISH Cook tomato, onion and garlic in small saucepan, stirring, about 10 minutes or until tomato has softened. Add sauce and vinegar; bring to a boil. Reduce heat; simmer, uncovered, stirring occasionally, about 10 minutes or until relish thickens. Cool 15 minutes.

per serving 6.2g total fat (1.1g saturated fat); 1981kJ (474 cal); 76.6g carbohydrate; 28.3g protein; 18.9g fibre

asian greens with kaffir lime rice

preparation time 15minutes cooking time 20 minutes serves 4

1 litre (4 cups) cold water

2 cups (400g) jasmine rice

4 fresh kaffir lime leaves, shredded

4cm piece fresh ginger (20g), chopped coarsely

2 fresh long red chillies, chopped coarsely

1 tablespoon sesame oil

1 large brown onion (200g), sliced thickly

200g green beans, trimmed

300g baby bok choy, quartered lengthways

100g snow peas, trimmed

150g oyster mushrooms, halved

100g enoki mushrooms, trimmed

⅓ cup (80ml) lime juice

2 tablespoons soy sauce

¼ cup coarsely chopped fresh coriander

1 Combine the water, rice, lime leaves, ginger and chilli in large saucepan with a tight-fitting lid; bring to a boil. Reduce heat, cook, covered, about 12 minutes or until all water is absorbed and rice is cooked. Do not remove lid or stir rice during cooking time. Remove from heat; stand, covered, 10 minutes before serving.

2 Meanwhile, heat half of the oil in wok; stir-fry onion until just softened. Add beans; stir-fry until just tender. Add bok choy, snow peas and mushrooms; stir-fry until bok choy just wilts. Add juice, sauce, coriander and remaining oil; stir-fry to combine.

3 Serve stir-fry with rice.

per serving 5.7g total fat (0.8g saturated fat); 1889kJ (452 cal); 85.7g carbohydrate; 12.9g protein; 7g fibre

vegetable cassoulet

preparation time 20 minutes (plus standing time) cooking time 1 hour 25 minutes serves 4

½ cup (100g) dried borlotti beans

½ cup (100g) dried great northern beans

2 teaspoons olive oil

4 shallots (100g), halved

3 cloves garlic, sliced thinly

2 medium carrots (240g), chopped coarsely

200g mushrooms, halved

1 cup (250ml) dry white wine

2 medium zucchini (240g), chopped coarsely

1½ cups (375ml) vegetable stock

700g bottled tomato pasta sauce

1 teaspoon finely chopped fresh thyme

BREAD TOPPING

1 tablespoon olive oil

1 small brown onion (80g), chopped finely

2 teaspoons finely grated lemon rind

1 clove garlic, crushed

2 teaspoons finely chopped fresh thyme

½ ciabatta (220g), diced into 2cm pieces

2 tablespoons coarsely chopped fresh flat-leaf parsley

1 Place beans in medium bowl, cover with water; stand overnight, drain. Rinse under cold water; drain. Place beans in medium saucepan of boiling water; return to a boil. Reduce heat; simmer, uncovered, about 15 minutes or until beans are just tender.

2 Preheat oven to moderate (180°C/160°C fan-forced).

3 Heat oil in large flameproof casserole dish; cook shallot, garlic, carrot and mushroom, stirring, until vegetables are just tender. Add wine; bring to a boil. Boil, uncovered, until liquid is reduced by half. Add zucchini, stock, sauce, thyme and drained beans; return to a boil. Remove from heat; transfer to oven. Cook, covered, 50 minutes.

4 Meanwhile, make bread topping.

5 Sprinkle cassoulet with bread topping; cook, uncovered, in oven about 10 minutes or until bread topping is browned.
BREAD TOPPING Heat oil in large frying pan; cook onion, stirring, until soft. Add rind, garlic, thyme and bread; cook, stirring, about 10 minutes or until bread browns lightly. Stir in parsley.
per serving 11.4g total fat (1.8g saturated fat); 2128kJ (509 cal); 68.3g carbohydrate; 22.7g protein; 19.6g fibre

CURRIES, SOUPS & STEWS
HEARTY MAINS LIKE THESE MADE WITHOUT MEAT? THEY'VE NEVER BEEN BETTER

As with the word casserole, tagine also has two different culinary meanings. Moroccan in origin, a tagine is the earthenware, cone-lidded vessel in which the spicy, fragrant North African stew with the same name is cooked.

vegetable tagine

preparation time 25 minutes cooking time 40 minutes serves 6

1 tablespoon coriander seeds

1 tablespoon cumin seeds

1 tablespoon caraway seeds

1 tablespoon vegetable oil

3 cloves garlic, crushed

2 large brown onions (400g), chopped finely

2 teaspoons sweet paprika

2 teaspoons ground ginger

1 tablespoon tomato paste

2 cups (500ml) water

2 x 400g cans diced tomatoes

600g pumpkin, chopped coarsely

8 yellow patty-pan squash (240g), quartered

200g baby green beans, trimmed, halved

300g can chickpeas, rinsed, drained

LEMON COUSCOUS

2 cups (400g) couscous

2 cups (500ml) boiling water

2 teaspoons coarsely grated lemon rind

2 teaspoons lemon juice

2 tablespoons coarsely chopped fresh flat-leaf parsley

1 Using mortar and pestle, crush seeds to a fine powder. Sift into small bowl; discard husks.

2 Heat oil in large saucepan; cook garlic and onion, stirring, until onion softens. Add crushed seeds and spices; cook, stirring, until fragrant.

3 Add paste, the water, undrained tomatoes and pumpkin; bring to a boil. Reduce heat; simmer, uncovered, 20 minutes. Stir in squash, beans and chickpeas; simmer, covered, about 10 minutes or until squash is tender.

4 Meanwhile, make lemon couscous.

5 Serve tagine with couscous.

LEMON COUSCOUS Combine couscous with the water in large heatproof bowl; cover, stand about 5 minutes or until water is absorbed, fluffing with fork occasionally. Stir in rind, juice and parsley.

per serving 5g total fat (0.8g saturated fat); 1643kJ (393 cal); 69.9g carbohydrate; 16.2g protein; 7.8g fibre

For a curry in a hurry, use a commercial curry paste. Try a small amount at first, then work up to adding more once you know the level of heat you can tolerate.

Serve with a Thai-style salad of snake beans, cabbage and thai basil.

yellow curry

preparation time 20 minutes cooking time 30 minutes serves 4

1⅔ cups (400ml) light coconut milk

1 cup (250ml) salt-reduced vegetable stock

1 large kumara (500g), chopped coarsely

200g green beans, trimmed

150g firm tofu, diced into 2cm cubes

2 tablespoons lime juice

¼ cup coarsely chopped fresh coriander

2 cups (400g) jasmine rice

YELLOW CURRY PASTE

1 teaspoon ground coriander

1 teaspoon ground cumin

1 teaspoon ground cinnamon

4cm piece fresh ginger (20g), chopped coarsely

2 cloves garlic, quartered

5 fresh long red chillies, chopped coarsely

5cm stick (10g) coarsely chopped fresh lemon grass

3 green onions, chopped finely

1 teaspoon salt

2 teaspoons curry powder

1 medium brown onion (150g)

1 Make yellow curry paste.

2 Cook half of the curry paste (freeze remaining paste for future use) in large saucepan, stirring, until fragrant. Add coconut milk and stock; bring to a boil. Reduce heat; simmer, stirring, 5 minutes. Add kumara; simmer, covered, about 10 minutes or until kumara is tender. Add beans, tofu and juice; cook, stirring, until beans are tender. Stir in coriander.

3 Meanwhile, cook rice in large saucepan of boiling water, uncovered, until just tender; drain.

4 Serve curry with rice topped with fresh coriander, if desired.
   YELLOW CURRY PASTE Dry-fry coriander, cumin and cinnamon in small frying pan, stirring, until fragrant. Blend or process spices with remaining ingredients until mixture forms a paste.
   per serving 3.5g total fat (3.5g saturated fat); 518kJ (124 cal); 20g carbohydrate; 3.4g protein; 1.2g fibre

SIMPLE MINESTRONE

Follow the recipe for vegetable and pasta soup, but use half a cup of uncooked risoni, orzo or soup pasta instead of the tagliatelle. Also, rather than finishing off the dish with the parsley and baby spinach, stir in a 400g can of rinsed and drained white beans when you add the pasta then, just before serving, a tablespoon of pesto.

CREAMY PASTA SAUCE

Make a delicious and quick sauce for penne, farfelle or little shells by following steps 2 and 3, right, adding perhaps a little more of each of the milk and stock until the desired consistency is reached. A tasty deviation can be achieved by using a green peppercorn dijon-style mustard instead of the wholegrain. Just before serving, stir a quarter of a cup of grated parmesan into the sauce.

54

vegetable and pasta soup

preparation time 15 minutes cooking time 25 minutes serves 4

1 tablespoon olive oil

1 large brown onion (200g), chopped finely

2 trimmed celery stalks (200g), chopped coarsely

2 medium carrots (240g), chopped coarsely

3 cloves garlic, crushed

1 teaspoon dried oregano

¼ teaspoon dried chilli flakes

1 litre (4 cups) boiling water

1 litre (4 cups) salt-reduced vegetable stock

125g tagliatelle

¼ cup coarsely chopped fresh flat-leaf parsley

60g baby spinach leaves, torn

1   Heat oil in large saucepan; cook onion, celery, carrot, garlic, oregano and chilli, stirring, until vegetables are just tender. Add the boiling water and stock; bring to a boil. Add pasta, reduce heat; simmer, uncovered, stirring occasionally, about 15 minutes or until pasta is tender. Stir in parsley.

2   Divide spinach among serving bowls; top with soup.
per serving 6.2g total fat (1.2g saturated fat); 861kJ (206 cal); 29.2g carbohydrate; 8.3g protein; 5g fibre

creamy leek, mushroom and baby pea pies

preparation time 15 minutes cooking time 25 minutes serves 4

You can buy mountain bread from most supermarkets. There are two varieties, white and wholemeal; either can be used for this recipe.

1 tablespoon olive oil

1 clove garlic, crushed

2 small leeks (400g), sliced thinly

300g mushrooms, chopped coarsely

2 tablespoons plain flour

½ cup (125ml) low-fat milk

½ cup (125ml) vegetable stock

1 cup (120g) frozen baby peas

1 tablespoon finely chopped fresh chives

1 tablespoon wholegrain mustard

4 slices white mountain bread, quartered

cooking-oil spray

1   Preheat oven to moderately hot (200°C/180°C fan-forced).

2   Heat oil in large saucepan; cook garlic and leek, stirring, until leek softens. Add mushrooms; cook, stirring, about 5 minutes or until mushrooms are tender.

3   Add flour; cook, stirring, 1 minute. Gradually stir in milk and stock; cook, stirring, until mixture boils and thickens slightly. Stir in peas, chives and mustard; cook about 2 minutes or until peas are tender.

4   Divide mixture among four 1¼-cup (310ml) ovenproof dishes; place dishes on oven tray. Top each with four scrunched up pieces of bread; spray bread lightly with oil. Cook, uncovered, about 10 minutes or until bread is browned lightly.
per serving 6.2g total fat (0.8g saturated fat); 832kJ (199 cal); 24.7g carbohydrate; 11g protein; 7.1g fibre

Chipotle is the name given to jalapeño chillies once they've been dried and smoked. They have a deep, intensely smoky flavour, rather than a searing heat.

black bean, corn and chipotle stew

preparation time 15 minutes (plus standing time) cooking time 1 hour serves 4

1½ cups (300g) dried black beans

2 chipotle chillies

½ cup (125ml) boiling water

1 tablespoon cumin seeds

2 trimmed corn cobs (500g)

2 teaspoons olive oil

1 large brown onion (200g), chopped finely

810g can crushed tomatoes

8 small white corn tortillas

SALSA

1 small red onion (100g), chopped coarsely

1 small tomato (90g), chopped coarsely

½ cup coarsely chopped fresh coriander

1 lebanese cucumber (130g), chopped coarsely

1 tablespoon olive oil

2 tablespoons lemon juice

1 Place beans in medium bowl, cover with water; stand overnight, drain. Rinse under cold water; drain. Place beans in medium saucepan of boiling water; return to a boil. Reduce heat; simmer, uncovered, about 15 minutes or until beans are just tender.

2 Preheat oven to moderately hot (200°C/180°C fan-forced).

3 Place chillies and the boiling water in small bowl; stand 15 minutes. Discard stalks; blend or process chilli and its soaking liquid until smooth.

4 Meanwhile, dry-fry cumin seeds in small frying pan, stirring, until fragrant.

5 Cook corn on heated oiled grill plate (or grill or barbecue) until browned lightly and just tender. When cool enough to handle, cut kernels from cobs with sharp knife.

6 Heat oil in large flameproof dish; cook onion, stirring, until soft. Add drained beans, chilli mixture, cumin, undrained tomatoes and half of the corn; bring to a boil. Cook, uncovered, in oven about 20 minutes or until sauce thickens.

7 Meanwhile, heat tortillas according to manufacturer's instructions.

8 Combine remaining corn with salsa ingredients in medium bowl.

9 Serve stew with tortillas and salsa.
per serving 10.4g total fat (1.3g saturated fat); 1839kJ (440 cal); 61.3g carbohydrate; 26.2g protein; 19.5g fibre

lentil and egg curry with lime pickle

preparation time 25 minutes cooking time 50 minutes serves 4

3 cardamom pods, bruised

1 teaspoon cumin seeds

1 teaspoon fennel seeds

2 teaspoons coriander seeds

1 teaspoon ground turmeric

1 teaspoon vegetable oil

1 medium brown onion (150g), sliced thinly

2 cloves garlic, crushed

3cm piece fresh ginger (15g), grated

1 fresh small red thai chilli, chopped finely

1½ cups (300g) brown lentils

1 cup (250ml) light coconut cream

1¾ cups (430ml) water

1 tablespoon lime juice

1½ cups (300g) basmati rice

2 hard-boiled eggs, quartered

¼ cup (75g) lime pickle

1 Dry-fry spices in small frying pan, stirring, until fragrant. Using mortar and pestle, crush spices to a fine powder.

2 Heat oil in large deep frying pan; cook onion, garlic, ginger and chilli, stirring, until onion softens. Add spices; cook, stirring, 1 minute. Add lentils, coconut cream and the water; bring to a boil. Reduce heat; simmer, covered, stirring occasionally, about 35 minutes or until lentils are tender. Stir in juice.

3 Cook rice in medium saucepan of boiling water, uncovered, until just tender; drain.

4 Serve curry with rice; top with eggs and lime pickle.
per serving 12.2g fat (6.9g saturated fat); 2420kJ (579 cal); 90.8g carbohydrate; 27.7g protein; 12.3g fibre

masala dosa with mint rasam

preparation time 20 minutes cooking time 35 minutes serves 4

2 large potatoes (600g), diced into 1.5cm pieces

1 tablespoon dried chickpeas

2 teaspoons vegetable oil

2 medium brown onions (300g), sliced thinly

1 teaspoon black mustard seeds

1 teaspoon ground turmeric

½ teaspoon dried chilli flakes

10 dried curry leaves

¾ cup (180ml) buttermilk

2 tablespoons finely chopped fresh coriander

4 chapatis

¼ cup (80g) mango chutney

MINT RASAM

2 teaspoons red lentils

2 teaspoons coriander seeds

½ teaspoon cumin seeds

½ teaspoon dried chilli flakes

2 medium tomatoes (300g), chopped coarsely

1 long green chilli, chopped finely

1 cup coarsely chopped fresh mint

¼ cup (50g) red lentils, extra

1 tablespoon tamarind paste

1¼ cups (310ml) water

1 Boil, steam or microwave potato until tender; drain.

2 Meanwhile, using mortar and pestle, lightly crush chickpeas.

3 Heat oil in large frying pan; cook onion, stirring, until soft. Add seeds, turmeric, chilli, curry leaves and crushed chickpeas; cook, stirring occasionally, over medium heat 10 minutes. Add potato and buttermilk; cook, covered, over low heat 5 minutes. Stir coriander into the potato masala.

4 Meanwhile, make mint rasam.

5 Warm chapatis, one at a time, in large heated frying pan; place a quarter of the potato masala on each chapati then roll to make filled masala dosa. Serve with mint rasam and chutney.

MINT RASAM Dry-fry lentils, seeds and chilli flakes in small frying pan, stirring, until fragrant. Using mortar and pestle, crush mixture finely. Place tomato, green chilli, mint and lentil mixture in medium saucepan; cook, stirring, 5 minutes. Add extra lentils, tamarind and the water; bring to a boil. Boil, uncovered, stirring occasionally, about 10 minutes or until lentils are soft and liquid has almost evaporated.

per serving 4.6g total fat (1.1g saturated fat); 1308kJ (313 cal); 53.4g carbohydrate; 14g protein; 10.2g fibre

STEAMED ARTICHOKES

Sometimes the simple things really
are the best. Trim the bases of 4 whole
globe artichokes so they sit flat; discard
the tough outer leaves then rinse
artichokes under cold water. Cook, in
single layer, in a covered steamer sitting
over a large saucepan of simmering water,
about 40 minutes or until the leaves pull
away easily and are tooth-tender. Drain
upside down then remove the hairy
choke with a spoon and discard it. Serve
as an entree, dipping leaves in a mixture
of melted butter and lemon juice.

OVEN-FRIED OKRA

Okra is a delicious but often ignored
vegetable because, if mishandled during
cooking, it releases a viscous property
that can be off-putting. Try this way of
cooking okra and we'll bet you'll be
converted: spray whole, untrimmed
okra with a little olive-oil spray then
place, on an oven tray, in a preheated
moderate (180°C/160°C fan-forced)
oven, turning once, about 20 minutes
or until okra are tender but crisp on the
outside. Serve as an accompaniment to
a vegetable curry and steamed rice.

62

artichoke fricassee

preparation time 30 minutes cooking time 25 minutes serves 4

1 medium lemon (140g), chopped coarsely

6 medium globe artichokes (1.2kg)

30g butter

2 cloves garlic, crushed

1 medium brown onion (150g), chopped coarsely

1 large leek (500g), sliced thickly

¼ cup (35g) plain flour

½ cup (125ml) vegetable stock

½ cup (125ml) water

1½ cups (375ml) skim milk

¾ cup (90g) frozen peas

1   Place lemon in large bowl half-filled with cold water. Discard outer leaves from artichokes; cut tips from remaining leaves, trim then peel stalks. Cut artichokes in half lengthways. Using small knife, remove and discard chokes. Place artichoke in lemon water.

2   Heat butter in large heavy-based saucepan; cook garlic, onion and leek, stirring occasionally, about 5 minutes or until vegetables just soften.

3   Add flour; cook, stirring, 1 minute. Gradually stir in stock, the water and milk, then add drained, rinsed artichokes; bring to a boil. Reduce heat; simmer, covered, about 15 minutes or until artichoke is just tender. Add peas; simmer, uncovered, until peas are heated through.

per serving 7.4g total fat (4.3g saturated fat); 920kJ (220 cal); 22g carbohydrate; 14.7g protein; 7.1g fibre

black-eyed beans, okra and kumara gumbo

preparation time 15 minutes (plus standing time) cooking time 1 hour 15 minutes serves 6

1 cup (200g) black-eyed beans

2 teaspoons olive oil

1 large brown onion (200g), chopped coarsely

3 cloves garlic, crushed

1 teaspoon dried thyme

2 teaspoons dried oregano

3 teaspoons ground fennel

1 teaspoon cayenne pepper

500g okra

600g kumara, chopped coarsely

2 x 425g cans crushed tomatoes

1 cup (250ml) water

1½ cups (300g) white long-grain rice

425g can baby corn, rinsed, drained

1   Place beans in medium bowl; cover with water, stand overnight, drain. Rinse under cold water; drain. Place beans in medium saucepan of boiling water; return to a boil. Reduce heat; simmer, uncovered, about 30 minutes or until beans are just tender.

2   Heat oil in large saucepan; cook onion and garlic, stirring, until onion softens. Add dried herbs and spices; cook, stirring, until fragrant.

3   Add drained beans, okra, kumara, undrained tomatoes and the water; bring to a boil. Reduce heat; simmer, uncovered, about 30 minutes or until vegetables are tender.

4   Meanwhile, cook rice in medium saucepan of boiling water, uncovered, until just tender; drain.

5   Stir corn into gumbo; cook, uncovered, until corn is heated through. Serve gumbo with rice.

per serving 3.9g total fat (0.5g saturated fat); 1881kJ (450 cal); 83.2g carbohydrate; 20.3g protein; 15.2g fibre

Dhansak is an Indian adaptation of a famous Parsi festive dish always consisting of several types of pulses and vegetables and served with rice.

vegetable dhansak

preparation time 40 minutes (plus standing time) **cooking time** 1 hour 30 minutes **serves 6**

1 large eggplant (500g), chopped coarsely

500g pumpkin, chopped coarsely

2 medium tomatoes (300g), peeled, chopped coarsely

1 large brown onion (200g), sliced thinly

3 cups (750ml) water

420g can chickpeas, drained, rinsed

400g can brown lentils, drained, rinsed

1 tablespoon garam masala

2 cups (400g) basmati rice

2 teaspoons vegetable oil

2 medium brown onions (300g), sliced thinly, extra

¼ cup firmly packed fresh coriander leaves

MASALA PASTE

3 dried small red chillies

2 long green chillies

2cm piece fresh ginger (10g), quartered

3 cloves garlic, quartered

½ cup loosely packed fresh coriander leaves

2 tablespoons hot water

1 Blend or process ingredients for masala paste until mixture forms a smooth paste.

2 Place eggplant, pumpkin, tomato, onion and the water in large saucepan; bring to a boil. Reduce heat; simmer, covered, 15 minutes, stirring occasionally. Drain vegetable mixture through sieve over large bowl; reserve 1½ cups of the cooking liquid, discard remainder.

3 Combine half of the chickpeas, half of the lentils and half of the vegetable mixture in another large bowl; mash lightly.

4 Dry-fry garam masala and masala paste in same cleaned pan, stirring, until fragrant. Add mashed and whole chickpeas, lentils and vegetable mixtures and reserved cooking liquid to pan; bring to a boil. Reduce heat; simmer, uncovered, 20 minutes, stirring occasionally.

5 Meanwhile, cook rice in large saucepan of boiling water until tender; drain.

6 Heat oil in medium saucepan; cook extra onion, stirring, about 10 minutes or until browned lightly. Sprinkle onion over dhansak; serve with rice and lemon wedges, if desired.
per serving 3.7g fat (0.6 saturated fat); 1614kJ (386 cal); 74.4g carbohydrate; 13.4g protein; 8.9g fibre

Vegetarian oyster sauce can be found in most supermarkets and Asian food stores.

Small red-brown sichuan peppercorns, also known as szechuan or chinese pepper, are actually not a member of the peppercorn family, but a berry from the prickly-ash tree having a distinctive peppery-lemon flavour and aroma.

vegetable dumplings in asian broth

preparation time 45 minutes cooking time 55 minutes serves 4

100g fresh shiitake mushrooms

2 green onions

1 medium brown onion (150g), chopped coarsely

1 medium carrot (120g), chopped coarsely

2 cloves garlic, chopped coarsely

2cm piece fresh ginger (10g), chopped coarsely

1 star anise

1 teaspoon sichuan peppercorns

¼ cup (60ml) soy sauce

2 tablespoons chinese cooking wine

4 coriander roots

1 teaspoon white sugar

1.5 litres (6 cups) water

800g bok choy

1cm piece fresh ginger (5g), extra, grated

1 clove garlic, extra, crushed

227g can water chestnuts, drained, chopped finely

1 egg white, beaten lightly

¼ cup (15g) stale breadcrumbs

2 tablespoons finely chopped fresh coriander

1 tablespoon vegetarian oyster sauce

20 wonton wrappers

100g enoki mushrooms, trimmed

1   Separate stems from caps of the shiitake mushrooms; reserve stems. Finely chop a quarter of the shiitake caps; slice remaining shiitake caps thinly. Coarsely chop white section of green onion. Thinly slice green section; reserve green section in small bowl.

2   Combine shiitake mushroom stems, white section of green onion, brown onion, carrot, garlic, ginger, star anise, peppercorns, soy sauce, wine, coriander roots, sugar and the water in large saucepan; bring to a boil. Reduce heat; simmer, uncovered, 45 minutes. Strain stock through muslin-lined sieve or colander into large bowl; discard solids. Return stock to same cleaned pan; bring to a boil. Reduce heat; simmer, covered.

3   Meanwhile, separate bases and leaves of bok choy. Finely chop half of the bases; discard remaining bases. Combine chopped bases with finely chopped shiitake mushrooms, extra ginger, extra garlic, water chestnuts, egg white, breadcrumbs, coriander leaves and oyster sauce in large bowl. Make dumplings by placing 1 heaped teaspoon of the mushroom mixture in centre of a wonton wrapper; brush around edges with a little water. Fold wrapper in half diagonally; pinch edges together to seal. Repeat with remaining mushroom mixture and wrappers.

4   Add sliced shiitake and enoki mushrooms to simmering stock; cook, uncovered, 5 minutes. Add dumplings; cook, uncovered, about 5 minutes or until dumplings are cooked through. Stir in bok choy leaves.

5   Divide soup among serving bowls; top with reserved sliced green onion.
per serving 1.6g total fat (0.2g saturated fat); 978kJ (234 cal); 40g carbohydrate; 11.6g protein; 6.8g fibre

Resembling a small folded pizza, the calzone is a southern Italian savoury turnover, filled with vegetables, herbs and cheese (almost always ricotta) then baked in a hot oven until golden brown.

ricotta and herb calzones

preparation time 30 minutes (plus standing time) cooking time 25 minutes (plus cooling time) serves 4

2 cups (300g) plain flour

1¼ teaspoons dry yeast (5g)

½ teaspoon salt

2 teaspoons olive oil

¾ cup (180ml) warm water

8 sun-dried tomatoes (50g)

1 clove garlic, crushed

¼ teaspoon dried chilli flakes

1 medium green capsicum (200g), sliced thinly

1 cup (200g) low-fat ricotta

⅓ cup (35g) coarsely grated low-fat mozzarella

⅓ cup (25g) finely grated parmesan

1 tablespoon coarsely chopped fresh oregano

1 tablespoon coarsely chopped fresh flat-leaf parsley

1 egg white, beaten lightly

1 Place flour, yeast and salt in large bowl; gradually stir in oil and the water, mix to a soft dough. Knead dough on floured surface about 5 minutes or until smooth and elastic. Place dough in large oiled bowl, turning dough once to coat in oil. Cover; stand in warm place about 1 hour or until dough doubles in size.

2 Meanwhile, place tomatoes in small heatproof bowl, cover with boiling water; stand 20 minutes, drain. Chop tomatoes coarsely.

3 Cook garlic, chilli and capsicum in medium heated, lightly oiled frying pan about 5 minutes or until capsicum has softened. Remove from heat; stir in tomato. Cool to room temperature. Combine capsicum mixture in medium bowl with cheeses and herbs.

4 Preheat oven to very hot (240°C/220°C fan-forced). Lightly oil two oven trays.

5 Turn dough onto floured surface; knead until smooth. Divide dough into quarters; using rolling pin, flatten dough and roll each quarter out to an 18cm round. Place a quarter of the cheese mixture in centre of dough; brush edge of dough with a little of the egg white; fold over to enclose filling, press edge to seal. Repeat with remaining dough, cheese mixture and egg white.

6 Place calzones onto prepared trays; brush with egg white and sprinkle with a little extra salt, if desired. Cut two slits in top of each calzone. Bake about 15 minutes or until browned lightly.
per serving 13.1g total fat (6.1g saturated fat); 1898kJ (454 cal); 60.6g carbohydrate; 22.6g protein; 5.5g fibre

GRILLS, ROASTS & BARBECUE
THESE VEGETARIAN RECIPES CAN STAND THE HEAT... EVEN OUT OF THE KITCHEN!

Quinoa, pronounced keen-wa, is the seed of a leafy plant similar to spinach. Like corn, rice, buckwheat and millet, quinoa is gluten-free and thought to be safe for consumption by people with coeliac disease. Its cooking qualities are similar to rice, and its delicate, slightly nutty taste and chewy texture make it a good partner for rich or spicy foods. You can buy it in most health food stores and some delicatessens; keep quinoa sealed in a glass jar under refrigeration because, like nuts and nut oils, it spoils easily.

barbecued fennel, orange and red onion with quinoa

preparation time 20 minutes cooking time 30 minutes serves 4

5 small fennel bulbs (1kg), trimmed, quartered lengthways

1 large red onion (300g), cut into thick wedges

2 tablespoons olive oil

2 cups (500ml) water

1 cup (170g) quinoa

½ cup (125ml) white wine vinegar

¼ cup coarsely chopped fresh dill

1 medium orange (240g), segmented

1 cup firmly packed fresh flat-leaf parsley leaves

1 Cook fennel and onion on heated oiled grill plate (or grill or barbecue), until vegetables are just tender, brushing with about half of the oil occasionally.

2 Meanwhile, bring the water to a boil in small saucepan. Add quinoa; reduce heat, simmer, covered, about 10 minutes or until water is absorbed. Drain.

3 Place fennel, onion and quinoa in large bowl with vinegar, dill, orange, parsley and remaining oil; toss gently.
per serving 10.2g total fat (1.4g saturated fat); 1208kJ (289 cal); 39.7g carbohydrate; 8.1g protein; 14g fibre

A CHEAT'S RISOTTO

Roast the pumpkin and garlic as
described in steps 1 and 2, right, but
do not process the vegetables. While
they're in the oven, make a quick risotto:
heat 1 litre water and 500ml vegetable
stock in a medium saucepan then stir
2 cups of arborio rice over heat in a
lightly oiled frying pan for 2 minutes
with the crushed garlic. Add the liquid
to the rice, in 1-cup batches, stirring
constantly between additions. When
risotto is tender, gently stir in pumpkin
pieces; serve sprinkled with chopped
fresh sage and grated parmesan.

BEETROOT AND ROAST
POTATO SALAD

Roast a kilo of oiled baby potatoes
as shown at right and toss them in a
large bowl with a rinsed and drained
850g can of baby beetroot, a ¼ cup
each of finely chopped chives and
flat-leaf parsley, a tablespoon of finely
chopped fresh dill and about ¼ cup of
a commercially made low-fat french
salad dressing. Separate the leaves of a
large red mignonette lettuce, tear them
roughly then toss into the potato and
beetroot salad to make an easy and very
colourful main course.

80

roasted pumpkin, sage and garlic pappardelle

preparation time 20 minutes cooking time 55 minutes serves 4

A wide, ribbon-like pasta with scalloped sides, pappardelle is sometimes sold as lasagnette or even lasagne. Any wide, long pasta can be used for this recipe.

1kg pumpkin, diced into 2cm pieces

4 cloves garlic, unpeeled

cooking-oil spray

500g pappardelle

1 cup (250ml) vegetable stock

375ml can light evaporated milk

1 teaspoon olive oil

⅓ cup loosely packed fresh sage leaves

⅓ cup (25g) finely grated parmesan

1   Preheat oven to hot (220°C/200°C fan-forced). Lightly oil oven tray.
2   Place pumpkin and garlic on tray; spray lightly with oil. Roast, uncovered, about 40 minutes or until pumpkin and garlic are tender. When cool enough to handle, peel garlic.
3   Meanwhile, cook pasta in large saucepan of boiling water, uncovered, until just tender.
4   Blend or process pumpkin and garlic with stock and milk until smooth.
5   Heat oil in medium saucepan; cook sage, stirring occasionally, until crisp. Remove from pan. Add pumpkin sauce to pan; stir until heated through. Stir in half of the cheese.
6   Drain pasta. Return pasta to large saucepan with pumpkin sauce; toss gently to combine. Divide pasta among serving bowls; sprinkle with sage and remaining cheese.
per serving 6.7g fat (2.7g saturated fat); 2600kJ (622 cal); 109.8g carbohydrate; 29.4g protein; 7.1g fibre

roast potato, onion and red capsicum salad

preparation time 15 minutes cooking time 40 minutes serves 4

1kg new potatoes, halved

1 medium red onion (170g), cut into thin wedges

1 large red capsicum (350g), chopped coarsely

2 teaspoons olive oil

80g baby rocket leaves

300g can red kidney beans, rinsed, drained

100g low-fat fetta, diced into 1cm pieces

2 tablespoons coarsely chopped fresh flat-leaf parsley

HONEY BALSAMIC DRESSING

1 tablespoon honey

2 teaspoons balsamic vinegar

2 teaspoons water

2 teaspoons olive oil

1   Preheat oven to hot (220°C/200°C fan-forced).
2   Combine potato, onion, capsicum and oil in large deep baking dish; roast, uncovered, about 40 minutes or until vegetables are browned and tender, stirring halfway through cooking time.
3   Place ingredients for honey balsamic dressing in screw-top jar; shake well.
4   Place roasted vegetables in large bowl with rocket, beans, cheese, parsley and dressing; toss gently to combine.
per serving 9.1g total fat (3g saturated fat); 1501kJ (359 cal); 50.5g carbohydrate; 17.9g protein; 9.4g fibre

This spin on stuffed capsicums sees the rice prepared as a dish in its own right before rather than during cooking time.

capsicums stuffed with pilaf

preparation time 20 minutes **cooking time** 55 minutes **serves 4**

2 teaspoons olive oil

1 medium red onion (170g), chopped finely

1 tablespoon slivered almonds

⅔ cup (130g) white long-grain rice

1 cup (250ml) water

2 tablespoons finely chopped dried apricots

¼ cup (35g) sun-dried tomatoes, chopped finely

¼ cup finely chopped fresh flat-leaf parsley

4 medium red capsicums (800g)

cooking-oil spray

ROASTED TOMATO SALAD

2 medium tomatoes (300g), cut into thick wedges

1 tablespoon apple cider vinegar

½ teaspoon cracked black pepper

1 teaspoon white sugar

1 cup firmly packed fresh flat-leaf parsley leaves

½ cup firmly packed fresh mint leaves

1 Preheat oven to moderately hot (200°C/180°C fan-forced).

2 Heat oil in medium saucepan; cook onion and nuts, stirring, until onion softens. Add rice; cook, stirring, 1 minute. Add the water; bring to a boil. Reduce heat; simmer, covered, about 15 minutes or until liquid is absorbed and rice is just tender. Stir in apricot, tomato and parsley.

3 Carefully cut tops off capsicums; discard tops. Discard seeds and membranes, leaving capsicum intact. Divide pilaf among capsicums; place capsicums on oven tray, spray with oil. Roast, uncovered, on oven tray 10 minutes. Cover loosely with foil; cook about 20 minutes or until capsicums are just soft.

4 Meanwhile, make roasted tomato salad.

5 Serve capsicums with roasted tomato salad.
   ROASTED TOMATO SALAD Combine tomato with vinegar, pepper and sugar in medium bowl. Drain; reserve liquid. Place tomato on oven tray; roast, uncovered, alongside capsicums about 10 minutes or until tomato just softens. Place tomato and reserved liquid in medium bowl with herbs; toss gently.
   per serving 5.7g total fat (0.6g saturated fat); 1087kJ (260 cal); 43.4g carbohydrate; 8.2g protein; 7.3g fibre

barbecued corn with chunky salsa and mexican rice

preparation time 20 minutes (plus refrigeration time) cooking time 30 minutes serves 4

4 untrimmed corn cobs (1.6kg)

2 teaspoons peanut oil

2 cloves garlic, crushed

1 small white onion (80g), chopped finely

1 small red capsicum (150g), chopped finely

1 fresh long red chilli, chopped finely

1½ cups (300g) white medium-grain rice

1 cup (250ml) vegetable stock

1 cup (250ml) water

CHUNKY SALSA

3 medium tomatoes (450g), chopped coarsely

1 small white onion (80g), chopped finely

¼ cup (60g) pickled jalapeño chillies

½ cup coarsely chopped fresh coriander

1 clove garlic, crushed

2 tablespoons lime juice

1   Gently peel husk down corn cob, keeping husk attached at base. Remove as much silk as possible then bring husk back over cob to re-wrap and enclose completely. Place corn in large bowl, add enough cold water to completely submerge corn.

2   Heat oil in medium saucepan; cook garlic, onion, capsicum and chilli, stirring, until onion softens. Add rice; cook, stirring, 1 minute. Add stock and the water; bring to a boil. Reduce heat; simmer, covered, about 20 minutes or until rice is just tender. Remove from heat; fluff rice with fork.

3   Meanwhile, drain corn. Cook corn on heated oiled grill plate (or grill or barbecue) about 25 minutes or until corn is tender, turning occasionally.

4   Combine ingredients for chunky salsa in medium bowl.

5   Serve corn with rice and salsa.
    per serving 6.7g total fat (0.9g saturated fat); 2541kJ (608 cal); 114g carbohydrate; 20.6g protein; 16.9g fibre

Use scissors to trim lasagne sheets to fit into your baking dish; you may only need three sheets in total.

roasted vegetable lasagne

preparation time 40 minutes (plus standing time) **cooking time** 1 hour **serves** 6

3 medium red capsicums (600g)

2 medium eggplants (600g), sliced thinly

2 tablespoons coarse cooking salt

2 medium zucchini (240g), sliced thinly

600g kumara, sliced thinly

cooking-oil spray

700g bottled tomato pasta sauce

4 fresh lasagne sheets

150g ricotta, crumbled

1 tablespoon finely grated parmesan

WHITE SAUCE

40g low-fat dairy-free spread

¼ cup (35g) plain flour

1½ cups (375ml) skim milk

2 tablespoons coarsely grated parmesan

1 Preheat oven to very hot (240°C/220°C fan-forced).

2 Quarter capsicums; discard seeds and membranes. Roast, uncovered, in very hot oven, skin-side up, about 5 minutes or until skin blisters and blackens. Cover capsicum pieces in plastic or paper for 5 minutes; peel away skin.

3 Reduce oven to moderately hot (200°C/180°C). Place eggplant in colander, sprinkle with salt; stand 20 minutes. Rinse eggplant under cold water; pat dry with absorbent paper.

4 Place eggplant, zucchini and kumara, in single layer, on oven trays; spray with oil. Roast, uncovered, about 15 minutes or until tender.

5 Meanwhile, make white sauce.

6 Oil deep rectangular 2.5-litre (10-cup) ovenproof dish. Spread 1 cup pasta sauce over base of prepared dish; top with half of the eggplant and half of the capsicum. Layer with lasagne sheet; top with ½ cup of the pasta sauce, ricotta, kumara and zucchini. Layer with another lasagne sheet; top with remaining pasta sauce, remaining eggplant and remaining capsicum. Layer remaining lasagne sheet over vegetables; top with white sauce, sprinkle with parmesan. Bake, uncovered, about 45 minutes or until browned lightly. Stand 5 minutes before serving with rocket salad.

WHITE SAUCE Melt spread in small saucepan, add flour; cook, stirring, until mixture thickens and bubbles. Remove from heat, gradually stir in milk; cook, stirring, until sauce boils and thickens. Remove from heat; stir in cheese.

per serving 9g fat (3.2g saturated fat); 1300kJ (311 cal); 44.1g carbohydrate; 14.2g protein; 8.1g fibre

A SAUCE FOR ALL SEASONS

This piquant combination of roasted vegetables can be treated in several ways: toss together with some olive oil then roast slightly longer, until tomato pieces no longer hold a shape. Serve as is with brown rice or green lentils; process briefly and eat as a chunky relish with cheese, pickles and rye bread, or use as an omelette filling; blend thoroughly with enough stock to make roasted vegie soup; cool then stir in double the amount of cayenne, a little finely chopped fresh coriander and seeded, chopped lebanese cucumber for a cooked salsa to snack on with corn chips – the possibilities are endless!

MUSHROOM MADNESS

While we've used flat and enoki mushrooms here, feel free to use whatever type you prefer or are in great supply – swiss brown, oyster, portobello, shiitake or even good-old garden-variety button. Also trying mixing two or three different kinds until you come up with a combination that seems truly perfect.

polenta-crusted eggplant
with roasted vegetable puree

preparation time 15 minutes cooking time 40 minutes serves 4

4 large egg tomatoes (360g), chopped coarsely

1 medium red onion (170g), quartered

1 small red capsicum (150g), quartered

1 small green capsicum (150g), quartered

¼ teaspoon cayenne pepper

1½ teaspoons curry powder

½ cup (75g) plain flour

2 egg whites

2 tablespoons soy sauce

1 cup (170g) polenta

2 tablespoons finely grated parmesan

1 medium eggplant (300g), cut into 12 slices

1 tablespoon olive oil

1   Preheat oven to moderate (180°C/160°C fan-forced).
2   Combine tomato, onion, capsicums, cayenne and ½ teaspoon of the curry powder on oven tray; roast, uncovered, about 30 minutes or until vegetables are tender. Cool 5 minutes. Blend or process vegetable mixture until smooth.
3   Meanwhile, place flour in medium bowl. Combine egg whites and sauce in another medium bowl. Combine polenta, cheese and remaining curry powder in separate medium bowl. Coat eggplant, one piece at a time, first in flour, then in egg mixture and then in polenta mixture.
4   Heat oil in medium frying pan; cook eggplant, in batches, until browned lightly both sides.
5   Serve eggplant with vegetable puree.
    per serving 7.3g total fat (1.5g saturated fat); 1354kJ (324 cal); 51.4g carbohydrate; 12.6g protein; 6.2g fibre

baked mushrooms with tomato and basil

preparation time 20 minutes cooking time 25 minutes serves 4

Serve with a fresh green salad dressed in a balsamic vinaigrette.

8 flat mushrooms (640g)

100g enoki mushrooms, chopped coarsely

3 green onions, chopped finely

125g grape tomatoes, halved

125g cream cheese, softened

½ cup coarsely chopped fresh basil

1 cup (70g) stale breadcrumbs

2 cups (500g) bottled tomato pasta sauce

⅓ cup (25g) finely grated parmesan

1   Preheat oven to moderately hot (200°C/180°C fan forced).
2   Remove stems from flat mushrooms; chop stems finely. Cook stems in medium heated lightly oiled frying pan, stirring, until tender. Stir in enoki, onion and tomato. Cool 10 minutes.
3   Combine mushroom mixture in medium bowl with cream cheese, basil and breadcrumbs; divide mixture among mushroom caps.
4   Place pasta sauce in medium baking dish; top with mushroom caps, sprinkle mushrooms with parmesan. Bake, uncovered, about 20 minutes or until mushroom caps are tender.
    per serving 14.5g total fat (8.2g saturated fat); 1275kJ (305 cal); 27.9g carbohydrate; 16.2g protein; 8.4g fibre

vegetarian kibbeh with fattoush

preparation time 30 minutes (plus standing time) cooking time 50 minutes serves 6

1 cup (160g) burghul

4 medium potatoes (800g), chopped coarsely

1 teaspoon ground allspice

1 tablespoon olive oil

3 large brown onions (600g), sliced thinly

1 tablespoon brown sugar

2 tablespoons water

¼ cup (40g) toasted almonds, chopped coarsely

⅓ cup finely chopped fresh flat-leaf parsley

FATTOUSH

6 small pocket pittas (330g), torn

3 lebanese cucumbers (390g), seeded, sliced thinly

5 small tomatoes (450g), chopped coarsely

4 green onions, sliced thinly

3 medium red radishes (105g), trimmed, sliced thinly

1½ cups firmly packed fresh flat-leaf parsley leaves

½ cup coarsely chopped fresh mint

2 teaspoons olive oil

¼ cup (60ml) lemon juice

1 Place burghul in medium bowl, cover with cold water; stand 30 minutes, drain.

2 Meanwhile, boil, steam or microwave potato until tender; drain. Mash potato in medium bowl with allspice.

3 Preheat oven to moderately hot (200°C/180°C fan-forced).

4 Heat oil in large frying pan; cook onion, stirring, about 10 minutes or until onion softens. Add sugar and the water; cook, stirring, over low heat, about 10 minutes or until onions are caramelised. Stir in nuts.

5 Add burghul and parsley to potato mixture; mash until smooth.

6 Lightly oil small baking dish. Using wet hands, press half of the potato mixture over base of dish; top with onion mixture. Press remaining potato mixture over onion mixture. Cook, uncovered, about 20 minutes or until browned lightly. Cut into wedges to serve.

7 Meanwhile, make fattoush.

8 Serve kibbeh with fattoush.
   FATTOUSH Place pitta, in single layer, on oven trays; toast in moderately hot oven about 10 minutes or until crisp. Combine pitta with remaining ingredients in medium bowl.
   per serving 10.4g total fat (1.3g saturated fat); 1831kJ (438 cal); 69.8g carbohydrate; 15.3g protein; 12.6g fibre

You can buy mountain bread from most supermarkets. There are two varieties, white and wholemeal, either can be used for this recipe.

You can make the patty mixture a day ahead; refrigerate, covered, until ready to use.

felafel rolls with tabbouleh and baba ghanoush

preparation time 25 minutes cooking time 45 minutes serves 4

1 teaspoon olive oil

1 medium brown onion (150g), chopped finely

1 clove garlic, crushed

2 teaspoons ground cumin

1 teaspoon ground coriander

½ teaspoon chilli powder

420g can chickpeas, rinsed, drained

1 cup coarsely chopped fresh flat-leaf parsley

2 teaspoons plain flour

2 teaspoons olive oil, extra

4 slices white mountain bread (100g)

BABA GHANOUSH

1 small eggplant (230g)

cooking-oil spray

2 teaspoons tahini

1 tablespoon lemon juice

1 tablespoon water

1 clove garlic, crushed

TABBOULEH

¼ cup (40g) burghul

¼ cup (60ml) boiling water

1 medium tomato (150g), seeded, chopped finely

2 cups coarsely chopped fresh flat-leaf parsley

2 tablespoons finely chopped fresh mint

2 tablespoons lemon juice

1 Preheat oven to moderately hot (200°C/180°C fan-forced).

2 Make baba ghanoush.

3 Meanwhile, heat oil in small frying pan; cook onion and garlic, stirring, until onion softens. Add spices; cook, stirring, until fragrant.

4 Blend or process chickpeas until chopped finely. Add onion mixture and parsley; blend until combined. Stir in flour.

5 Using hands, shape mixture into eight patties. Place on lightly oiled oven tray; brush with extra oil. Cook, uncovered, in oven about 20 minutes or until browned both sides.

6 Meanwhile, make tabbouleh.

7 Roll each piece of mountain bread into a cone; secure with a toothpick. Divide tabbouleh and patties among cones. Serve with baba ghanoush.

BABA GHANOUSH Pierce eggplant all over with fork. Place eggplant on lightly oiled oven tray; spray with oil. Roast, uncovered, about 40 minutes or until tender. When cool enough to handle, peel eggplant. Blend or process eggplant flesh with remaining ingredients until smooth.

TABBOULEH Combine burghul and the boiling water in medium heatproof bowl; cover, stand 10 minutes, fluffing occasionally with fork. Stir in remaining ingredients.

per serving 7g total fat (0.9g saturated fat); 1012kJ (242 cal); 32.7g carbohydrate; 11.2g protein; 11.2g fibre

It goes without saying that if you have a grapevine in your yard and the season is right, most certainly use its fresh leaves. Clean under cold water before plunging them, one or two at a time, briefly into boiling water, to make them pliable enough to roll.

Packaged grapevine leaves in brine can be found in most Middle Eastern food stores. You need one 200g packet for this recipe.

burghul-stuffed vine leaves with yogurt dip

preparation time 25 minutes (plus standing time) **cooking time** 15 minutes **serves** 6

1 cup (160g) burghul

1 cup (250ml) boiling water

1 tablespoon olive oil

1 green onion, chopped finely

¼ cup (35g) toasted slivered almonds

2 tablespoons finely chopped raisins

2 tablespoons finely chopped fresh mint

1 tablespoon finely chopped fresh coriander

1 tablespoon finely chopped fresh flat-leaf parsley

2 teaspoons ground cinnamon

2 teaspoons finely grated lemon rind

1 tablespoon lemon juice

40 grapevine leaves in brine (200g), rinsed, drained

YOGURT DIP

¾ cup (200g) low-fat yogurt

1 tablespoon finely chopped fresh mint

1 tablespoon finely chopped fresh coriander

1 teaspoon lemon juice

5cm piece fresh ginger (25g), grated

1 Combine burghul and the boiling water in medium heatproof bowl. Cover; stand 5 minutes. Stir in oil, onion, nuts, raisins, herbs, cinnamon, rind and juice.

2 Line base of large bamboo steamer with about 10 vine leaves.

3 Place one of the remaining leaves, vein-side up, on board; place 1 tablespoon of the burghul mixture in centre of leaf. Fold in two opposing sides; roll to enclose filling. Repeat with remaining leaves and burghul mixture.

4 Place rolls, in single layer, on leaves in steamer. Steam, covered, over wok of simmering water about 15 minutes or until rolls are heated through.

5 Meanwhile, combine ingredients for yogurt dip in small bowl.

6 Serve rolls with yogurt dip
per serving 7g total fat (0.8g saturated fat); 757kJ (181 cal); 21.7g carbohydrate; 7.5g protein; 7g fibre

STEAMS, BRAISES & BAKES
THREE METHODS WHERE LOW-FAT VEGETARIAN COOKING REALLY COMES INTO ITS OWN

STEAMS, BRAISES & BAKES

THE SWEETEST LEEKS

A member of the onion family, the leek resembles a green onion but is much larger and more subtle in flavour. Baby or pencil leeks are beautifully tender and are superb steamed then eaten as a cold entree, either drizzled with a classic Sicilian aquadolce (literally sour-sweet) dressing or sprinkled with a mixture of toasted breadcrumbs and sieved hard-boiled egg (the French polonaise sauce). Large leeks are good, cleaned and chopped, used as an ingredient in casseroles and soups.

SPAGHETTI 'N' NEATBALLS

Have a little play with our recipe at right and gently poach the balls of spinach mixture in an increased amount of the tomato and herb sauce (or any good prepared pasta sauce with which you have an affinity). Cook 125g spaghetti for each serving and serve with meatless "neatball" sauce, sprinkled with parmesan and shredded fresh basil.

100

braised balsamic leeks with creamy polenta

preparation time 30 minutes cooking time 30 minutes serves 4

2 large leeks (1kg), trimmed

2 teaspoons olive oil

1 clove garlic, crushed

1 large red capsicum (350g), sliced thinly

2 tablespoons balsamic vinegar

⅓ cup firmly packed fresh flat-leaf parsley leaves

CREAMY POLENTA

2 cups (500ml) water

1 cup (250ml) vegetable stock

1¼ cups (310ml) skim milk

1 cup (170g) polenta

2 tablespoons finely grated parmesan

1 Halve leeks crossways; cut halves into quarters lengthways.

2 Heat oil in large saucepan; cook garlic, stirring, until fragrant. Add leek and capsicum; cook, covered, stirring occasionally, about 20 minutes or until leek softens. Add vinegar; cook, uncovered, stirring occasionally, until almost all liquid has evaporated.

3 Meanwhile, make creamy polenta.

4 Stir parsley into leek mixture. Serve with creamy polenta.
   CREAMY POLENTA Combine the water, stock and 1 cup of the milk in medium saucepan; bring to a boil. Gradually add polenta to liquid, stirring constantly. Reduce heat; simmer, stirring, about 10 minutes or until polenta thickens. Stir in cheese and remaining milk just before serving.
   per serving 5.3g total fat (1.4g saturated fat); 1129kJ (270 cal); 42.6g carbohydrate; 12.7g protein; 6.8g fibre

steamed spinach dumplings with fresh tomato and herb sauce

preparation time 30 minutes (plus standing time) cooking time 20 minutes serves 4

2 x 250g packets frozen spinach, thawed

200g ricotta

1 clove garlic, crushed

1 egg white

1 tablespoon plain flour

¼ cup (20g) finely grated parmesan

1½ cups (110g) stale breadcrumbs

¼ teaspoon ground nutmeg

1 tablespoon finely chopped fresh chives

2 tablespoons finely grated parmesan, extra

FRESH TOMATO AND HERB SAUCE

½ cup (125ml) dry white wine

4 medium tomatoes (600g), chopped finely

2 tablespoons finely chopped fresh flat-leaf parsley

1 teaspoon white sugar

1 Squeeze excess liquid from spinach. Combine spinach in large bowl with ricotta, garlic, egg white, flour, parmesan, breadcrumbs, nutmeg and chives; roll level tablespoons of the mixture into balls. Place balls, in single layer, about 2cm apart in baking-paper-lined bamboo steamer fitted over large saucepan of boiling water. Steam, covered, about 10 minutes or until dumplings are hot.

2 Meanwhile, make fresh tomato and herb sauce.

3 Serve dumplings with sauce and extra parmesan.
   FRESH TOMATO AND HERB SAUCE Bring wine to a boil in medium saucepan. Reduce heat; simmer, uncovered, until reduced by half. Add tomato; return to a boil. Boil, uncovered, about 10 minutes or until thickened slightly. Stir in parsley and sugar.
   per serving 10.2g total fat (5.5g saturated fat); 1233kJ (295 cal); 25.7g carbohydrate; 19.4g protein; 9.3g fibre

A traditional sukiyaki pan can be purchased from Japanese food or homeware shops, however, an electric frying pan is a good substitute. Only about a quarter of the sukiyaki is cooked at a time, and individual portions are eaten, in batches, by diners who dip the hot food into a bowl containing a lightly beaten raw egg (which cooks on contact). Customarily, any remaining broth and egg are mixed together in each diner's bowl then served over steamed rice at the end of the meal.

vegetarian sukiyaki

preparation time 15 minutes **cooking time** 15 minutes **serves** 4

440g fresh udon noodles

8 fresh shiitake mushrooms

4 green onions, cut into 3cm lengths

100g baby spinach leaves

230g can bamboo shoots, drained

½ small chinese cabbage (350g), chopped coarsely

100g enoki mushrooms, trimmed

1 small leek (200g), chopped coarsely

2 medium carrots (240g), sliced thickly

350g firm tofu, diced into 2cm pieces

4 eggs

BROTH

1 cup (250ml) soy sauce

½ cup (125ml) cooking sake

½ cup (125ml) mirin

1 cup (250ml) water

½ cup (110g) white sugar

1 Rinse noodles under hot water; drain. Cut into random lengths.

2 Combine ingredients for broth in medium saucepan; cook over medium heat, stirring, until sugar dissolves.

3 Meanwhile, remove and discard shiitake stems; cut a cross in the top of caps.

4 Arrange all ingredients, except eggs, on platters or in bowls. Place broth in medium bowl.

5 Break eggs into individual bowls; beat lightly.

6 Pour broth into sukiyaki (or electric frying pan) pan. Heat pan on portable gas cooker at the table; cook a quarter of the noodles and a quarter of the remaining ingredients in broth, uncovered, until just tender. Dip cooked ingredients into egg before eating. Repeat process until all the remaining noodles and ingredients are cooked.

per serving 11.9g total fat (2.5g saturated fat); 2232kJ (534 cal); 65.8g carbohydrate; 29g protein; 9.4g fibre

braised root vegetables with gremolata

preparation time 15 minutes cooking time 50 minutes serves 4

1 tablespoon olive oil

2 cloves garlic, crushed

2 large parsnips (700g), sliced thickly

2 large carrots (360g), chopped coarsely

2 medium turnips (450g), chopped coarsely

1 cup (250ml) vegetable stock

3 medium beetroot (500g), cut into thin wedges

¼ cup (60ml) lemon juice

GREMOLATA

1 cup finely chopped fresh flat-leaf parsley

1 tablespoon finely grated lemon rind

1 clove garlic, crushed

1 Preheat oven to moderately hot (200°C/180°C fan-forced).
2 Heat half of the oil in large frying pan; cook garlic, parsnip, carrot and turnip, in batches, stirring, until vegetables are browned lightly. Add stock; bring to a boil. Reduce heat; simmer, covered, about 40 minutes or until vegetables are tender.
3 Meanwhile, combine remaining oil and beetroot in medium shallow baking dish; cook, uncovered, about 40 minutes or until beetroot is tender.
4 Combine ingredients for gremolata in small bowl.
5 Stir juice and beetroot into braised vegetables. Divide vegetables among serving plates; top with gremolata. Serve with couscous, if desired.

per serving 5.4g total fat (0.8g saturated fat); 899kJ (215 cal); 33g carbohydrate; 7.9g protein; 13.2g fibre

steamed asian greens with scrambled tofu

preparation time 20 minutes (plus standing time) cooking time 30 minutes serves 4

600g soft silken tofu

1 tablespoon sesame oil

350g broccolini, chopped coarsely

800g chinese water spinach, chopped coarsely

170g asparagus, trimmed, halved

2 medium red onions (340g), chopped finely

1 fresh long red chilli, chopped finely

⅓ cup (80ml) vegetarian oyster sauce

PALM SUGAR DRESSING

⅓ cup (80ml) lime juice

1 tablespoon grated palm sugar

1 tablespoon soy sauce

1 Pat tofu dry with absorbent paper; chop coarsely. Spread tofu, in single layer, on absorbent-paper-lined tray; stand 30 minutes.
2 Heat 3 teaspoons of the oil in wok; stir-fry tofu until all liquid has been absorbed and tofu has browned lightly. Remove from wok; cover to keep warm.
3 Meanwhile, boil, steam or microwave broccolini, spinach and asparagus, separately, until tender; drain.
4 Heat remaining oil in same cleaned wok; stir-fry onion and chilli until onion softens. Add sauce, stir-fry, 2 minutes.
5 Place ingredients for palm sugar dressing in screw-top jar; shake well.
6 Place tofu, onion mixture and half of the dressing in large bowl; toss gently.
7 Divide vegetables among serving plates; drizzle with remaining dressing. Top with scrambled tofu.

per serving 16.3g total fat (2.2g saturated fat); 1434kJ (343 cal); 17.1g carbohydrate; 31.3g protein; 14.1g fibre

THE ESSENCE OF GREMOLATA

As it has become more fashionable, gremolata has morphed into myriad guises well removed from its original form. Once just a simple garnish strewn over steaming osso buco so the scent of its combined parsley, garlic and lemon rind would excite the palate, today it can be made from any number of aromatic ingredients and served with many different dishes. Olive, rocket, coriander, rosemary, breadcrumb, shallot, orange and lime, even chilli, gremolatas can be seen sprinkled over everything from soups to steamed vegetables..

LARB TOFU

Make a thai larb salad starting with steps 2 and 3 at left. While tofu is draining, chop one red onion, enough coriander to make half a cup, about 2cm lemon grass stalk, and two small thai chillies. Toss these in a large bowl with the browned tofu and a dressing made from two tablespoons lemon juice, one teaspoon grated palm sugar, one tablespoon soy sauce and dollop of sambal oelek. Serve spooned into whole chinese cabbage leaves

105

steamed gow gees with miso dipping sauce

preparation time 40 minutes cooking time 30 minutes makes 28

2 teaspoons peanut oil

2 cloves garlic, crushed

5cm piece fresh ginger (25g), grated

1 fresh small red thai chilli, chopped finely

150g oyster mushrooms, chopped finely

2 small carrots (140g), chopped finely

3 green onions, sliced thinly

½ cup (40g) bean sprouts

100g soft tofu, chopped finely

227g can water chestnuts, drained, chopped finely

¼ cup finely chopped fresh coriander

28 gow gee wrappers

MISO DIPPING SAUCE

1 tablespoon white miso paste

1 tablespoon soy sauce

1 tablespoon lime juice

1 green onion, sliced thinly

2 tablespoons water

1 Heat oil in large frying pan; cook garlic, ginger and chilli until fragrant. Add mushrooms, carrot, onion, sprouts, tofu and chestnuts; cook, stirring occasionally, about 5 minutes or until vegetables soften. Remove from heat; stir in coriander. Cool 10 minutes.

2 Place 1 level tablespoon of the mixture on centre of each wrapper. Brush edges with a little water; fold wrapper over to completely enclose filling, pressing edges together to seal.

3 Place gow gees, in single layer, about 1cm apart in baking-paper-lined steamer fitted over large saucepan of boiling water; steam, covered, about 10 minutes or until gow gees are heated through.

4 Meanwhile, combine ingredients for miso dipping sauce in small bowl.

5 Serve gow gees with dipping sauce and steamed asian greens, if desired.
   per gow gee 0.5g total fat (0.1g saturated fat); 159kJ (38 cal); 6g carbohydrate; 0.9g protein; 0.8g fibre

mushroom, pea and artichoke risotto

preparation time 15 minutes cooking time 45 minutes serves 4

3 cups (750ml) vegetable stock

2 cups (500ml) water

2 teaspoons olive oil

1 medium brown onion (150g), chopped finely

2 cloves garlic, crushed

2 cups (400g) arborio rice

200g mushrooms, chopped coarsely

1 cup (250ml) dry white wine

¼ cup coarsely chopped fresh flat-leaf parsley

340g jar quartered marinated artichokes hearts, drained

1 cup (120g) frozen peas

⅔ cup (50g) coarsely grated parmesan

1 Place stock and the water in medium saucepan; bring to a boil. Reduce heat; simmer, covered.

2 Heat oil in large saucepan; cook onion and garlic, stirring, until soft. Add rice and mushrooms; stir to coat in onion mixture. Stir in wine; cook, stirring, until wine is absorbed. Add ½ cup of the simmering stock mixture; cook, stirring, over low heat until stock is absorbed. Continue adding stock, in ½-cup batches, stirring, until stock is absorbed after each addition. Total cooking time should be about 35 minutes or until rice is tender.

3 Stir in remaining ingredients; cook, uncovered, until peas are tender.
   per serving 9.8g total fat (3.8g saturated fat); 2358kJ (564 cal); 87.3g carbohydrate; 19.2g protein; 4.6g fibre

POTSTICKERS

Change the wrapper and the cooking method and these gow gees become potstickers, also known as gyoza in Japanese cooking. Follow our recipe to the end of step 2, replacing the gow gee with round wonton wrappers. Heat a tablespoon of vegetable oil in a large frying pan, add the filled wrappers and fry on one side only until browned lightly. Add a cup of cold water to the pan; bring to a boil. Cover, reduce heat; steam about 15 minutes or until most of the water evaporates. Uncover; cook until remaining water evaporates. Combine ¼ cup each of red rice vinegar and soy sauce with a teaspoon of chilli oil in a small bowl to make a dipping sauce for the potstickers.

DEEP-FRIED RISOTTO BALLS

Here's a great way to recycle any leftover risotto: shape a heaped tablespoon of the risotto mixture into a ball; press a piece of mozzarella into centre of each ball, roll to enclose. Coat risotto balls in packaged breadcrumbs. Heat vegetable oil in large saucepan; deep-fry risotto balls, no more than three at a time, until browned and heated through. Serve on their own or with a fresh basil and tomato sauce, if desired.

STEAMS, BRAISES & BAKES

113

ALLSPICE also known as pimento or jamaican pepper; so-named because it tastes like a combination of nutmeg, cumin, clove and cinnamon.

ARTICHOKES

globe large flower-bud of a member of the thistle family, having tough petal-like leaves; edible in part when cooked.

hearts tender centre of the globe artichoke. Artichoke hearts can be harvested fresh from the plant or purchased in brine canned or in glass jars.

BAKING POWDER a raising agent consisting mainly of two parts cream of tartar to one part bicarbonate of soda (baking soda).

BAMBOO SHOOTS the tender shoots of bamboo plants, available in cans; must be drained and rinsed before use.

BEANS

black an earthy-flavoured dried bean also known as turtle beans or black kidney beans.

black-eyed also known as black-eyed peas, are the dried seed of a variant of the snake or yard bean.

borlotti also known as roman beans, they can be eaten fresh or dried. Are a pale pink or beige colour with darker red spots.

lima large, flat, kidney-shaped, beige, dried and canned beans. Also known as butter beans.

snake long (about 40cm), thin, round, fresh green beans. Asian in origin, with a taste similar to green or french beans. Used most frequently in stir-fries, they are also called yard-long beans.

sprouts also known as bean shoots; tender new growths of assorted beans and seeds germinated for consumption as sprouts.

BEETROOT also known as red beets or just beets; a firm, round root vegetable.

BOK CHOY also known as bak choy, pak choy or chinese white cabbage; has a mild mustard taste. Use both stems and leaves. *Baby bok choy* is smaller and more tender, and often cooked whole.

BROCCOLINI a cross between broccoli and chinese kale; is milder and sweeter than broccoli. Substitute chinese broccoli (gai larn) or common broccoli.

BREADS

chapati a popular unleavened Indian bread, chapati is used to scoop up pieces of food in lieu of cutlery. Made from whole-wheat flour, salt and water, and dry-fried on a tawa (a cast-iron griddle). Available from Indian food stores and supermarkets.

ciabatta in Italian, the word means slipper, which is the traditional shape of this popular crisp-crusted white bread.

mountain bread a thin, dry, soft-textured bread that can be used for sandwiches or rolled up and filled with your favourite filling. Available from health food stores and supermarkets.

pitta also known as lebanese bread. Is sold in large, flat pieces that separate into two thin rounds. Also available in small thick pieces called pocket pitta.

sourdough so-named, not because it's sour in taste, but because it's made by using a small amount of 'starter dough', which contains a yeast culture, mixed into flour and water. Part of the resulting dough is then saved to use as the starter dough next time.

tortilla thin, round unleavened bread originating in Mexico. Made from either wheat flour or corn.

BURGHUL also known as bulghur wheat; hulled steamed wheat kernels that, once dried, are crushed into various size grains. Not the same as cracked wheat. Used in Middle-Eastern dishes such as kibbeh and tabbouleh.

BUTTERMILK originally the liquid left after cream was separated from milk, today it is commercially made similarly to yogurt.

CAPSICUM also known as bell pepper or pepper. Discard seeds and membranes before use.

CARAWAY SEEDS a member of the parsley family, available in seed or ground form.

CARDAMOM native to India; can be purchased in pod, seed or ground form. Has a distinctive aromatic, sweetly rich flavour, and is one of the world's most expensive spices.

CHEESE

cheddar, low-fat a semi-hard cow-milk cheese. We used one with a fat content of less than 7%.

fetta crumbly goat- or sheep-milk cheese with a sharp, salty taste.

haloumi a firm, cream-coloured sheep-milk cheese; somewhat like a minty, salty fetta in flavour. Can be grilled or fried, briefly, without breaking down.

mozzarella soft, spun-curd cheese traditionally made from water-buffalo milk.

ricotta soft, white, cow-milk cheese. Is a sweet, moist cheese with a slightly grainy texture and a fat content of around 8.5%.

romano a hard cheese made from cow or sheep milk. Straw-coloured and grainy in texture, it's mainly used for grating. Parmesan can be substituted.

parmesan also known as parmigiano, parmesan is a hard, grainy cow-milk cheese.

CHERVIL also known as cicily; mildly fennel-flavoured herb with curly dark-green leaves.

CHICKPEAS also called channa, garbanzos or hummus; a sandy-coloured, irregularly round, legume, often used in Latin and Mediterranean cooking.

CHILLI

cayenne pepper a thin-fleshed, long, extremely hot, dried red chilli, usually purchased ground; both arbol and guajillo chillies are the fresh sources for cayenne.

chipotle chillies hot, dried, smoked jalapeños.

jalapeños fairly hot, green chillies, available bottled in brine or fresh from specialty greengrocers.

thai red small, medium hot, and bright red in colour.

CHINESE CABBAGE also known as peking cabbage, wong bok or petsai. Elongated in shape with pale green, crinkly leaves.

CHINESE COOKING WINE made from rice, wheat, sugar and salt, with 13.5% alcohol; available from Asian food stores. Mirin or sherry can be substituted.

CHINESE WATER SPINACH also known as swamp spinach, water convulvus, ung choy, ung tsai and kang kong. Both the long pointed leaves and hollow stems are used like spinach in soups and stir-fries. Wash thoroughly before use. Not related to common spinach, however, spinach or watercress may be substituted, if necessary. Available from Asian food shops.

COOKING-OIL SPRAY we used a cholesterol-free cooking spray made from canola oil.

CORIANDER also known as cilantro or chinese parsley; bright-green-leafed herb with a pungent flavour. Both stems and roots are used in Thai cooking.

GLOSSARY

COUSCOUS a fine, grain-like cereal product, originally from North Africa; made from semolina.

CUMIN also known as zeera; related to the parsley family. Has a spicy, nutty flavour. Available in seed form or dried and ground.

CURLY ENDIVE also known as frisee, a curly-leafed green vegetable, mainly used in salads.

CURRANTS, DRIED tiny, almost black, raisins so-named after a grape variety that originated in Corinth, Greece. Available from supermarkets.

DAIKON also known as white radish. Used in Japanese cooking; has a sweet flavour without the bite of the red radish.

EGGPLANT also known as aubergine; ranging in size from tiny to very large and in colour from pale green to deep purple, eggplant has an equally wide variety of flavours.

EVAPORATED MILK unsweetened canned milk from which water has been extracted by evaporation.

FENNEL also known as finocchio or anise; can be eaten raw or braised or fried. Also the name given to dried seeds having a licorice flavour.

FIVE-SPICE POWDER a fragrant mixture of ground cinnamon, cloves, star anise, sichuan pepper and fennel seeds.

GAI LARN also known as chinese kale or chinese broccoli; appreciated more for its stems than its coarse leaves.

GALANGAL also known as ka, a rhizome with a hot ginger-citrusy flavour; used similarly to ginger and garlic. Fresh ginger can be substituted for fresh galangal, but the flavour of the dish will not be the same.

GARAM MASALA a blend of roasted, ground spices, including cardamom, cinnamon, cloves, coriander, fennel and cumin. Black pepper and chilli can be added for a hotter version.

GINGER

fresh also known as green or root ginger; the thick gnarled root of a tropical plant.

ground also known as powdered ginger; cannot be substituted for fresh ginger.

pickled pink pickled paper-thin shavings of ginger in a mixture of vinegar, sugar and natural colouring. Available, packaged, from Asian grocery stores.

GOW GEE WRAPPERS spring roll, egg pastry sheets or wonton wrappers can be substituted.

HARISSA a sauce or paste made from dried red chillies, garlic, oil and sometimes caraway seeds.

KAFFIR LIME LEAVES also known as bai magrood; look like two glossy, dark green leaves joined end to end, forming an hourglass shape. Sold fresh, dried or frozen; the dried leaves are less potent so double the number if you substitute them for fresh leaves. A strip of fresh lime peel may be substituted for each kaffir lime leaf.

KECAP MANIS a dark, thick, sweet soy sauce used in most South-East Asian cuisines. The soy's sweetness is derived from either molasses or palm sugar.

KUMARA Polynesian name of orange-fleshed sweet potato often confused with yam.

LAMINGTON PAN 20cm x 30cm slab cake pan, 3cm deep.

LEBANESE CUCUMBER short, slender and thin-skinned; this variety is also known as the european or burpless cucumber.

LEMON GRASS a tall, clumping, lemon-smelling and tasting, sharp-edged grass; the white lower part of the stem is chopped and used in Asian cooking or for tea.

LOW-FAT DAIRY-FREE SPREAD we used a polyunsaturated, cholesterol-free, reduced-fat diet spread.

MISO is usually termed red or white, although 'red' miso is dark brown in colour and 'white' is more the colour of weak tea. Made in Japan, miso is a paste made from cooked, mashed, salted and fermented soy beans. Also known as misi.

MIRIN a japanese champagne-coloured cooking wine made of glutinous rice and alcohol expressly for cooking and should not be confused with sake; there is also a seasoned sweet mirin called manjo mirin.

MUSHROOMS

enoki clumps of long, thin stems with tiny, snowy white caps and a delicate fruit flavour.

flat large, flat mushrooms with a rich earthy flavour, ideal for filling and barbecuing. They are sometimes misnamed field mushrooms, which are wild mushrooms.

oyster also known as abalone; grey-white mushroom shaped like a fan. Has a smooth texture and subtle, oyster-like flavour.

shiitake when fresh are also known as chinese black, forest or golden oak mushrooms; are large and meaty and have the earthiness and taste of wild mushrooms. When dried, they are known as donko or dried chinese mushrooms; rehydrate before use.

swiss brown light to dark brown mushrooms with full-bodied flavour.

NOODLES

bean thread noodles known as wun sen or cellophane or glass noodles because when cooked they become transparent. White in colour, very delicate and fine. Must be soaked to soften before use; using them deep-fried requires no pre-soaking.

fresh egg noodles also known as ba mee or yellow noodles. Range in size from very fine strands to wide, thick spaghetti-like pieces as thick as a shoelace.

fresh rice also known as ho fun, khao pun, sen yau, pho or kway tiau. Purchased in various widths or large sheets, which are cut into the desired width. Chewy and pure white, they do not need pre-cooking before use.

fried crispy egg noodles packaged (most commonly a 100g packet) already deep-fried.

soba thin spaghetti-like pale brown noodle from Japan made from buckwheat and varying proportions of wheat flour.

udon available fresh and dried, these japanese broad white wheat noodles are similar to the ones in homemade chicken noodle soup.

NORI a type of dried seaweed used in Japanese cooking. Sold in thin sheets, plain or toasted.

NUTMEG the dried nut of a tropical tree; available in ground form, or you can grate your own with a fine grater.

OKRA also known as bamia or lady fingers; has a green, ridged, oblong pod with a furry skin. Is used to thicken stews.

ONIONS

green also known as scallion or, incorrectly, shallot; an immature onion picked before the bulb has formed, having a long, bright-green edible stalk.

red also known as spanish, red spanish or bermuda onion; a sweet-flavoured, large, purple-red onion.

PAPAYA also known as pawpaw, is a large, pear-shaped red-orange tropical fruit. Sometimes used unripe (green) in cooking.

PAPRIKA ground, dried red capsicum (bell pepper), available sweet or hot.

PARSLEY, FLAT-LEAF also known as continental or italian parsley.

PASTA
angel hair also known as barbina.
pappardelle a wide, ribbon-like pasta with scalloped edges.
risoni also known as risi; small, rice-shaped pasta very similar to another small pasta, orzo.
tagliatelle long, flat strips of durum wheat pasta, narrower and thinner than fettuccine.

PATTY-PAN SQUASH also known as crookneck or custard marrow pumpkins; a round, slightly flat summer squash yellow to pale green in colour and having a scalloped edge. Harvested young, it has firm white flesh and a distinct flavour.

POLENTA also known as cornmeal. A flour-like cereal made of dried corn (maize) and sold ground in several different textures. Also the name of the dish made from it.

RICE
arborio small, round grain rice well-suited to absorb a large amount of liquid; especially suitable for risottos.
basmati a white, fragrant long-grained rice. Should be washed several times before cooking.
jasmine fragrant long-grained rice; white rice can be substituted but will not taste the same.
risoni see under "pasta".

ROCKET also known as arugula, rugula and rucola; a peppery-tasting green leaf that can be used similarly to baby spinach leaves, eaten raw in salad or used in cooking. *Baby rocket leaves* are both smaller and less peppery.

SAFFRON stigma of a member of the crocus family, available in strands or ground form; imparts a yellow-orange colour to food once infused. Should be stored in the freezer.

SAKE Japan's favourite rice wine; is used in cooking, marinating and as part of dipping sauces. If sake is unavailable, dry sherry, vermouth or brandy can be used as a substitute.

SHALLOTS also called french shallots, golden shallots or eschalots, small, elongated, brown-skinned members of the onion family.

SICHUAN PEPPERCORNS also known as szechuan or chinese pepper, is native to the Sichuan province of China. A mildly-hot spice from the prickly ash tree. Although it is not related to the peppercorn family, the small, red-brown aromatic sichuan berries look like black peppercorns, and have a distinctive peppery-lemon flavour and aroma.

SNOW PEAS also called mange tout ('eat all'). *Snow pea tendrils*, the growing shoots of the plant, are sold by greengrocers.

SPINACH also known as english spinach and, incorrectly, silverbeet. Tender green leaves are good uncooked in salads or added to soups, stir-fries and stews just before serving.

STAR ANISE a dried, star-shaped pod whose seeds have an astringent aniseed flavour; used to favour stocks and marinades.

STOCK available in cans, bottles or tetra packs. Stock cubes or powder can be used. As a guide, 1 teaspoon of stock powder or 1 small crumbled stock cube mixed with 1 cup (250ml) water will give a fairly strong stock. Be aware of the salt and fat content of stock cubes and powders and prepared stocks.

SUGAR we used coarse, granulated table sugar, also known as crystal sugar, unless otherwise specified.

brown a soft, fine sugar retaining molasses for colour and flavour.
caster also known as superfine or finely granulated table sugar.
palm sugar also known as nam tan pip, jaggery, jawa or gula melaka; made from the sap of the sugar palm tree. Light brown to black in colour and usually sold in rock-hard cakes; if unavailable substitute with brown sugar.

SUGAR SNAP PEAS also known as honey snap peas; fresh, small pea that can be eaten whole, pod and all, similarly to snow peas.

SUMAC a purple-red, astringent ground spice; adds a tart, lemony flavour to dips and dressings. Found in Middle-Eastern food stores. *Substitute:* ½ teaspoon lemon pepper *plus* ⅛ teaspoon five-spice *plus* ⅛ teaspoon allspice *equals* ¾ teaspoon sumac.

SWEDES also known as rutabaga, swedes have a yellow skin and look similar to turnips, although a little larger in size.

TAHINI sesame seed paste available from Middle-Eastern food stores; most often used in hummus, baba ghanoush and other Lebanese-style recipes.

TAMARIND the tamarind tree can grow as high as 25 metres. It produces clusters of brown 'hairy' pods, each of which is filled with seeds and a viscous pulp, that are dried and pressed into the blocks of tamarind found in Asian food stores. Gives a sweet-sour, slightly astringent taste to food. Is used mainly as a souring agent in marinades, pastes, sauces and dressings.

TOFU also known as bean curd, an off-white, custard-like product made from the milk of crushed soy beans; comes fresh as soft or firm, and processed as fried or pressed dried sheets. Silken tofu refers to the method by which it is made – where it is strained through silk.

TOMATO
egg also called plum or roma; are smallish, oval-shaped tomatoes used in Italian cooking or salads.

teardrop small yellow pear-shaped tomatoes.

TURMERIC also known as kamin, is a rhizome related to galangal and ginger and must be grated or pounded to release its acrid aroma and pungent flavour. Known for the golden colour it imparts to the dishes of which it's a part, fresh turmeric can be substituted with the more common dried powder (use 2 teaspoons of ground turmeric plus a teaspoon of sugar for every 20g of fresh turmeric called for in a recipe).

VINEGAR
balsamic authentic only from the province of Modena, Italy; made from a regional wine of white Trebbiano grapes specially processed then aged in antique wooden casks, which gives it a exquisite pungent flavour.
cider from fermented apples.
malt made from fermented malt and beech shavings.
red wine based on fermented red wine.
rice a colourless vinegar made from fermented rice, sugar and salt. Also known as seasoned rice vinegar. Sherry can be substituted.

WATER CHESTNUTS resembles a chestnut in appearance, hence the English name. They are small brown tubers with a crisp, white, nutty-tasting flesh. Their crunchy texture is best experienced fresh, however, canned water chestnuts are more easily obtained and can be kept about a month, once opened, under refrigeration.

WONTON WRAPPERS also known as wonton skins; made of flour, egg, and water, they come in varying thicknesses. Found in the refrigerated section of Asian grocery stores.

YAKI-NORI a type of dried seaweed used in Japanese cooking as a flavouring, garnish or for sushi. Sold in thin sheets.

ZUCCHINI also known as courgettes; small green, yellow or white vegetable belonging to the squash family and having edible flowers.

MEASURES

One Australian metric measuring cup holds approximately 250ml; one Australian metric tablespoon holds 20ml; one Australian metric teaspoon holds 5ml.

The difference between one country's measuring cups and another's is within a two- or three-teaspoon variance, and will not affect your cooking results. North America, New Zealand and the United Kingdom use a 15ml tablespoon.

All cup and spoon measurements are level. The most accurate way of measuring dry ingredients is to weigh them. When measuring liquids, use a clear glass or plastic jug with the metric markings.

We use large eggs with an average weight of 60g.

DRY MEASURES

METRIC	IMPERIAL
15g	½oz
30g	1oz
60g	2oz
90g	3oz
125g	4oz (¼lb)
155g	5oz
185g	6oz
220g	7oz
250g	8oz (½lb)
280g	9oz
315g	10oz
345g	11oz
375g	12oz (¾lb)
410g	13oz
440g	14oz
470g	15oz
500g	16oz (1lb)
750g	24oz (1½lb)
1kg	32oz (2lb)

LIQUID MEASURES

METRIC	IMPERIAL
30ml	1 fluid oz
60ml	2 fluid oz
100ml	3 fluid oz
125ml	4 fluid oz
150ml	5 fluid oz (¼ pint/1 gill)
190ml	6 fluid oz
250ml	8 fluid oz
300ml	10 fluid oz (½ pint)
500ml	16 fluid oz
600ml	20 fluid oz (1 pint)
1000ml (1 litre)	1¾ pints

LENGTH MEASURES

METRIC	IMPERIAL
3mm	⅛in
6mm	¼in
1cm	½in
2cm	¾in
2.5cm	1in
5cm	2in
6cm	2½in
8cm	3in
10cm	4in
13cm	5in
15cm	6in
18cm	7in
20cm	8in
23cm	9in
25cm	10in
28cm	11in
30cm	12in (1ft)

OVEN TEMPERATURES

These oven temperatures are only a guide for conventional ovens.
For fan-forced ovens, check the manufacturer's manual.

	°C (CELSIUS)	°F (FAHRENHEIT)	GAS MARK
Very slow	120	250	½
Slow	150	275-300	1-2
Moderately slow	160	325	3
Moderate	180	350-375	4-5
Moderately hot	200	400	6
Hot	220	425-450	7-8
Very hot	240	475	9

CONVERSION CHART

INDEX

ARE YOU MISSING SOME COOKBOOKS?

The Australian Women's Weekly Cookbooks are available from bookshops, cookshops, supermarkets and other stores all over the world. You can also buy direct from the publisher, using the order form below.

TITLE	RRP	QTY	TITLE	RRP	QTY
100 Fast Fillets	£6.99		Just For One	£6.99	
A Taste of Chocolate	£6.99		Just For Two	£6.99	
After Work Fast	£6.99		Kids' Birthday Cakes	£6.99	
Beginners Cooking Class	£6.99		Kids Cooking	£6.99	
Beginners Simple Meals	£6.99		Kids' Cooking Step-by-Step	£6.99	
Beginners Thai	£6.99		Low-carb, Low-fat	£6.99	
Best Food Fast	£6.99		Low-fat Food for Life	£6.99	
Breads & Muffins	£6.99		Low-fat Meals in Minutes	£6.99	
Brunches, Lunches & Treats	£6.99		Main Course Salads	£6.99	
Cafe Classics	£6.99		Mexican	£6.99	
Cafe Favourites	£6.99		Middle Eastern Cooking Class	£6.99	
Cakes Bakes & Desserts	£6.99		Midweek Meals in Minutes	£6.99	
Cakes Biscuits & Slices	£6.99		Mince in Minutes	£6.99	
Cakes Cooking Class	£6.99		Mini Bakes	£6.99	
Caribbean Cooking	£6.99		Moroccan & the Foods of North Africa	£6.99	
Casseroles	£6.99		Muffins, Scones & Breads	£6.99	
Casseroles & Slow-Cooked Classics	£6.99		New Casseroles	£6.99	
Cheap Eats	£6.99		New Curries	£6.99	
Cheesecakes: baked and chilled	£6.99		New French Food	£6.99	
Chicken	£6.99		New Salads	£6.99	
Chinese and the foods of Thailand, Vietnam, Malaysia & Japan	£6.99		One Pot	£6.99	
Chinese Cooking Class	£6.99		Party Food and Drink	£6.99	
Chocs & Treats	£6.99		Pasta Meals in Minutes	£6.99	
Cookies & Biscuits	£6.99		Quick & Simple Cooking	£6.99	
Cooking Class Cake Decorating	£6.99		Rice & Risotto	£6.99	
Cupcakes & Fairycakes	£6.99		Saucery	£6.99	
Detox	£6.99		Sauces Salsas & Dressings	£6.99	
Dinner Lamb	£6.99		Sensational Stir-Fries	£6.99	
Dinner Seafood	£6.99		Simple Healthy Meals	£6.99	
Easy Comfort Food	£6.99		Simple Starters Mains & Puds	£6.99	
Easy Curry	£6.99		Slim	£6.99	
Easy Midweek Meals	£6.99		Soup	£6.99	
Easy Spanish-Style	£6.99		Stir-fry	£6.99	
Food for Fit and Healthy Kids	£6.99		Superfoods for Exam Success	£6.99	
Foods of the Mediterranean	£6.99		Tapas Mezze Antipasto & other bites	£6.99	
Foods That Fight Back	£6.99		Thai Cooking Class	£6.99	
Fresh Food Fast	£6.99		Traditional Italian	£6.99	
Fresh Food for Babies & Toddlers	£6.99		Vegetarian Meals in Minutes	£6.99	
Good Food for Babies & Toddlers	£6.99		Vegie Food	£6.99	
Great Kids' Cakes (May 08)	£6.99		Wicked Sweet Indulgences	£6.99	
Greek Cooking Class	£6.99		Wok Meals in Minutes	£6.99	
Grills	£6.99				
Healthy Heart Cookbook	£6.99				
Indian Cooking Class	£6.99				
Japanese Cooking Class	£6.99		TOTAL COST	£	

Mr/Mrs/Ms _____

Address_____ Postcode _____

Day time phone _____ email* (optional) _____

I enclose my cheque/money order for £ _____

or please charge £ _____

to my: ☐ Access ☐ Mastercard ☐ Visa ☐ Diners Club

Card number | | | | | | | | | | | | | | | | |

Expiry date _____ 3 digit security code *(found on reverse of card)* _____

Cardholder's name_____ Signature _____

To order: Mail or fax – photocopy or complete the order form above, and send your credit card details or cheque payable to: Australian Consolidated Press (UK), ACP Books, 10 Scirocco Close, Moulton Park Office Village, Northampton NN3 6AP. phone (+44) (0)1604 642200 fax (+44) (0)1604 642300 email books@acpuk.com or order online at www.acpuk.com
Non-UK residents: We accept the credit cards listed on the coupon, or cheques, drafts or International Money Orders payable in sterling and drawn on a UK bank. Credit card charges are at the exchange rate current at the time of payment. **Postage and packing UK:** Add £1.00 per order plus £1.75 per book. **Postage and packing overseas:** Add £2.00 per order plus £3.50 per book. All pricing current at time of going to press and subject to change/availability. **Offer ends 31.12.2009**
* By including your email address, you consent to receipt of any email regarding this magazine, and other emails which inform you of ACP's other publications, products, services and events, and to promote third party goods and services you may be interested in.

TEST KITCHEN
Food director Pamela Clark
Associate food editor Alexandra Somerville
Home economists Ariane Bradshaw, Nicole Jennings, Elizabeth Macri, Sharon Reeve, Susie Riggall, Jessica Sly, Kirrily Smith, Kate Tait, Kellie-Marie Thomas, Helen Webster

ACP BOOKS
General manager Christine Whiston
Editorial director Susan Tomnay
Creative director Hieu Chi Nguyen
Senior editor Wendy Bryant
Director of sales Brian Cearnes
Marketing manager Bridget Cody
Business analyst Rebecca Varela
Operations manager David Scotto
Production manager Victoria Jefferys
International rights enquires Laura Bamford
lbamford@acpuk.com

ACP Books are published by ACP Magazines a division of PBL Media Pty Limited
Group publisher, Women's lifestyle Pat Ingram
Director of sales, Women's lifestyle Lynette Phillips
Commercial manager, Women's lifestyle Seymour Cohen
Marketing director, Women's lifestyle Matthew Dominello
Public relations manager, Women's lifestyle Hannah Deveraux
Creative director, Events, Women's lifestyle Luke Bonnano
Research Director, Women's lifestyle Justin Stone
ACP Magazines, Chief Executive officer Scott Lorson
PBL Media, Chief Executive officer Ian Law

Produced by ACP Books, Sydney.
Published by ACP Books, a division of ACP Magazines Ltd, 54 Park St, Sydney; GPO Box 4088, Sydney, NSW 2001. phone (02) 9282 8618 fax (02) 9267 9438. acpbooks@acpmagazines.com.au www.acpbooks.com.au
Printed by Goodmanbaylis Ltd in the UK.

Australia Distributed by Network Services, phone +61 2 9282 8777 fax +61 2 9264 3278 networkweb@networkservicescompany.com.au
United Kingdom Distributed by Australian Consolidated Press (UK), phone (01604) 642 200 fax (01604) 642 300 books@acpuk.com
New Zealand Distributed by Netlink Distribution Company, phone (9) 366 9966 ask@ndc.co.nz
South Africa Distributed by PSD Promotions, phone (27 11) 392 6065/6/7 fax (27 11) 392 6079/80 orders@psdprom.co.za
Canada Distributed by Publishers Group Canada phone (800) 663 5714 fax (800) 565 3770 service@raincoast.com

A catalogue record for this book is available from the British Library.
ISBN 978-1-86396-479-1.
© ACP Magazines Ltd 2006
ABN 18 053 273 546
This publication is copyright. No part of it may be reproduced or transmitted in any form without the written permission of the publishers.
First published 2006. Reprinted 2006, 2007, 2008.

Scanpan cookware is used in the AWW Test Kitchen.
Send recipe enquiries to: askpamela@acpmagazines.com.au